A R T

IN
UNEXPECTED
PLACES

COMMISSIONER'S MESSAGE

Article 83 of the Constitution of New Hampshire includes phrases that speak directly to all of us who are concerned with the cultural health of our state:

"Knowledge and learning, generally diffused through a community, being essential to the preservation of a free government…it shall (therefore) be the duty of the legislators and magistrates, in all future periods of this government, to cherish the interest of literature and the sciences…to encourage private and public institutions, rewards and immunities for the promotion of agriculture, arts, science…."

In the spirit of the founding fathers, our legislators of this century have responded to Article 83 by establishing the Department of Libraries, Arts and Historical Resources to identify, preserve, and promote the interests of literature, New Hampshire's heritage, and the visual and performing arts.

Within this cultural agency, the New Hampshire State Council on the Arts administers the splendid Percent for Art Program. The provisions of RSA 19-A:9, the legislation which governs the Council, establishes a non-lapsing art fund to bring the work of professional artists into the State of New Hampshire's buildings. The vision of the makers of our constitution is thus amplified and made real by today's farsighted citizen legislators.

The program is celebrating 10 years of bringing significant art works by the artists of New Hampshire and the northeast to the people of New Hampshire. We look ahead to many more years in which the arts community will continue to make lasting contributions that enhance our New Hampshire way of life.

Shirley Gray Adamovich,
Commissioner
Department of Libraries,
Arts and Historical Resources

The artist of ancient Greece, Rome and Egypt worked with the knowledge that his art would be common property as part of the churches and government buildings which formed the center of daily life in the urban centers. The anonymous sculptors who created images of Christian iconography in stone worked closely with the architects of the medieval cathedrals. The alliance of artist and architect continued through the Renaissance, but the public role of the artist declined in the seventeenth, eighteenth and nineteenth centuries. Sculpture, in particular, fell to a position of relative unimportance. If it had any role at all, it was generally as ornament for gardens or parks.

There was, however, a strong regard for commemorating public figures, particularly military heroes and their victories. Public statuary of the nineteenth and early twentieth century was intended to be a symbol of civic and national virtue and thus an elevating experience for the public. In the words of Oliver Larkin, "Legislators up and down the land were in a mood to commission stone reminders of those who had made the republic." In New Hampshire, citizens and elected officials erected statues of John P. Hale, Daniel Webster, John Stark and Franklin Pierce on the plaza before the State House in Concord, while from their pedestals, Generals Stark and Pulaski maintain an eternal vigilance in Manchester.

It was during the period of the 1930's, when Federal support for public art was significant, that the General Pulaski monument was created by Manchester artist, Lucien H. Gosselin. The sculpture was funded through a collaboration of private citizens, the City of Manchester, and the State of New Hampshire.

Federal funds channeled through the Works Progress Administration supported many forms of art during the troubled decade of 1930.

Under the directorship of Omer T. Lassonde of Manchester, Federal funds were used to subsidize the work of printmakers and painters. Herbert Waters was paid to teach landscape and art history in the public schools in Concord and Bradford and also to experiment with wood engraving and linoleum block printing techniques. Gladys Brannigan produced four large murals depicting the history of local events such as the visits of George Washington and General Lafayette, and historical Portsmouth buildings for the Portsmouth Junior High School auditorium. Among other New Hampshire artists were Albert Quigley, Francis W. P. Tolman, and Alice Ericson Cosgrove, who later became an artist for the New Hampshire State Planning and Development Commission. These artists primarily depicted scenes in New Hampshire which reflected the American faith in hard work as a solution for all problems.

By the mid-sixties, a new generation of American artists, and several of the older sculptors, began to exhibit work devoid of humanist concerns and dependent on a highly rational regard for materials and construction methods derived from industrial techniques. They questioned the function of the pedestal and many preferred to do away with it altogether, allowing the work to interact directly with the spectator in a mutual space. The choice of materials expanded, with painted steel and aluminum becoming more and more evident. This change was due both to aesthetic reasons, bright, primary colors were finding increasing favor, and economic reasons, sheet metal was less costly than the traditional method of casting in bronze. A new service industry was created, the art fabricator who understood both the techniques of handling, crafting and finishing large pieces of metal, and could also provide expertise in transport and installation.

The major monuments of the Western world have resulted from the formation of a coalition between artist and patron, someone who was willing to assume the burden of cost. Wealthy individuals with a predilection for immortality have always played a role as backer for the artist. The state and church also provided the funds necessary for the creation of monumental art.

Commercial interests have been involved with arts for many years, but in recent decades their participation has intensified. The Federal government is no longer concerned only with building monuments for the nation's capitol. Its Arts-in-Architecture Program commissions art for new federal construction throughout the country. The National Endowment for the Arts actively supports and aids the placing of public art through several grants programs. Many states and cities have public art programs that set aside a percent of construction costs for art.

In metropolitan areas such as Cambridge, Massachusetts, art has been incorporated into public transportation systems as subway revitalization projects created new lines from the city's center to outlying areas. Numerous artists have created art as diverse as mobiles from high tech materials, cast bronze figures, poetry imbedded in flooring brick, stained glass, and clay wall tiles fabricated by a professional artist who used imagery produced by children from the area in which the station was built. Several museums have run projects which enable the artist to work with local industries which provide materials and manpower for works created to be placed in their own cities. Hawaii, the first state in the nation to establish a Percent for Art Program, set aside one percent of state construction budgets for commissioning or purchase of artwork, a precedent which has found ever wider acceptance in government practice. Government on all levels, business large and small, universities and other educational institutions, all have become leading patrons of the arts as commissioning agents.

The expansion of opportunity for patronage in the last two decades is unparalleled. It has resulted in a huge stabile by the late Alexander Calder for Grand Rapids, Michigan, works by George Sugarman for Akron, Ohio and Baltimore, Maryland, and a massive baseball bat by Claes Oldenburg, commissioned by the federal office of the General Services Administration for the City of Chicago, home of the Cubs and the White Sox, to mention only a few pieces in the Midwest alone. In fact, the city without some monumental work of art in a public site is becoming the exception rather than the rule. The patronage that makes public art a reality is often a partnership of government, business and private citizens. The result is the planning and production of more urban and sometimes rural monuments than at any other time in the history of the nation, and a greater possibility that art and the people will have the chance to interact in daily life.

The art commissioned by the State of New Hampshire for its public buildings not only enhances those centers of government, but also makes them an open gallery for the art of our time. They become places in which art and architecture work together to bring about an environment designed to meet the needs and interests of its citizens. Many works of art were commissioned and all were selected for a particular site. All were chosen for their ability to stimulate the hearts and minds of the spectator. The selections of type of artwork and imagery were made through a collaboration of building users and arts professionals.

The growing art collection for the people of New Hampshire is for all who enjoy the arts. But it also serves a greater need, the eternal affirmation of commitment to hard work, faith, patience, imagination and aesthetic integrity—all those factors which take place in the act of creation and assure the survival of human values. The works of art in New Hampshire's public buildings symbolize the spirit of free inquiry and creative integrity which are so vital to modern society and the duty of governments to protect and promote the right of the creative individual to live and work in freedom.

Robert M. Doty, Director
The Currier Gallery of Art
from 1977 to 1987

The first 10 years of the Percent for Art Program were a period of risk taking and problem solving that led everyone who participated to learn and grow. Each player or set of players in the art selection process had to stretch the limits of his/her own knowledge, shift perceptions, develop negotiating and communicating skills, and create solutions for new and uncharted territories.

Artists had to learn to work with committees, grapple with budget limitations, and find creative solutions not only in making their art or craft, but also in fulfilling their role as artist on construction sites. In some cases, artists had to learn about fund-raising and politics.

Art experts on the Art Selection Committees had to consider new public responsibilities in selecting the artists. Users of the buildings on Site Advisory Committees were challenged by new visions as they reviewed works by the 500 artists in the Artists' Slide Registry. In the process of sifting through the images, both committees learned more about what kind of art they liked and why. They also grew to respect each other's choices.

Construction foremen had to accommodate unusual projects within their spaces and work with artists who were accustomed to working alone and independently. Architects, as they collaborated with artists, had to learn restraint to keep from taking over the artists' designs and making them their own. State agencies responsible for housing the art had to learn new skills while cooperating with the arts agency to provide lighting, manpower and materials for installations of artwork. Maintenance crews within state buildings inherited new kinds of objects with unfamiliar and challenging curatorial needs.

The state arts agency had to hone negotiating skills in the political arena and even within the governing board itself, when the concept that "art is for everyone" was challenged by a mandate to provide art for the New Hampshire State Prison. With each project, arts administrators had to invent new ways of meeting the sometimes conflicting needs of artists, art selectors, and board members as the process took shape.

As everyone boarded the same train it sometimes seemed that everyone was getting off at a different station to reach the same destination.

The evolution of the Percent for Art Program began with the drafting of House Bill 430, which proposed that a percentage of state construction appropriations be used to purchase artwork for state buildings and facilities. Nine sponsors signed on to the bill: James V. Bibbo, Jr; Mary B. Chambers; Marshall French; Ruth Griffin; Mary Louise Hancock; Peter Hildreth; Elaine Krasker; Paul LaMott; and Vesta M. Roy. The sponsors originally had hoped that the percentage for art would be one percent. Jim Bibbo said of the process, "It was tough. But, anything out of my committee was tough." Eventually, the one percent became one-half percent.

Thanks to the hard work of the sponsors and many others who gave testimony at hearings, the bill passed into law in 1979. When the law was passed, New Hampshire became one of only 13 states with similar legislation. Each of these states had to experiment with finding their own ways of implementing these new laws. New Hampshire's law allows a small percentage of funds to be used to purchase art and historical objects for existing state buildings as well as to commission works for new buildings. The law restricts certain entities from generating funds: e.g., the University System of New Hampshire and self-liquidating projects. The responsibility for managing the program was given to the New Hampshire Commission on the Arts.

The fledgling program was watched anxiously by diverse groups within the state, some of whom had never collaborated before. As Elaine Krasker (a prime sponsor of the legislation) and Calvin J. Libby (Co-chairman of the Percent for Art Task Force) wrote in 1979, "Just how this art is selected is...a matter of great interest and concern of many artists, craftsmen, state agencies, legislators and the New Hampshire Commission on the Arts."

The Commission established a Task Force to hammer out guidelines for the art selection process. Attending these early meetings were representatives from the Arts Commission, Citizens for the Arts, League of New Hampshire Craftsmen, New Hampshire Art Association, New Hampshire Chapter of American Institute of Architects, New Hampshire Department of Public Works, New Hampshire Historical Society, and the New Hampshire Visual Arts Coalition. In April of 1980 the administrative rules for the State Art Fund were adopted.

Two committees were to develop the art plan for each building: A Site Advisory Committee to represent the views and needs of the resident agency or agencies and an Art Selection Committee of arts professionals to determine the scope, direction, and particular aesthetic needs of each site. Together they would make the choices. The Art Selection Committee would relay decisions to the Arts Commission, which would issue artists' contracts and submit them to the Governor and Executive Council for approval.

A pilot project, funded at $25,000, was designed for the first building, Health and Welfare (later renamed Health and Human Services). Committee members felt awed by the responsibility with which they were entrusted. Each person experienced an added concern since private decisions would be scrutinized by the public. After two years of deliberations over the needs of the agency, how to create harmony within the space, the dilemma of having 17 spaces which could benefit from artwork, and a budget which could not possibly "do it all," and furthermore, resolving what types of images and what kinds of materials would be most appropriate, the group tentatively made its choices. Much to the surprise of the individuals present, there was unanimous agreement on the artists to recommend. It had been a long process, one where no one had been certain whether or not the process would, in fact, work.

From 1979 to 1989, 45 arts professionals and 100 representatives from 13 buildings struggled with these questions. Seventy-two artists prepared sketches, models, and ideas for competitions. Of these, 29 were commissioned to create site-specific works. Additional works from 45 other artists were purchased for permanent installations. The state's collection grew to 120 artworks chosen for particular sites. Paintings; drawings; photographs; prints; tapestries; architectural constructions in glass and in wood; sculptures in bronze, mosaic, Coreten steel, granite, travertine, aluminum, native woods; and painted and clay tile murals make up this far-flung collection, spread among 13 sites.

The artwork for each site is distinctive and represents the diversity of viewpoints of those who participated in the choices. Within each building there is a cohesiveness of imagery which gives the building a special identity.

A unique opportunity arose for the Arts Commission when new prison construction provided enough funds to introduce an additional means of circulating artwork around the state. The Arts Commission met the challenge of choosing artwork for the public spaces in the prison while channeling remaining funds into the purchase of a touring collection representing artists who, in the main, were not represented in the state's site-related collection. Known as Arts Bank, the collection traveled 5,000 miles to 22 public buildings throughout New Hampshire. Arts Bank exhibited 181 artworks from 103 artists.

From the beginning, the state arts agency was sensitive to its public responsibility for state funds. It was aware that the public sometimes worried about the cost of artwork, for example, for a large outdoor sculpture; but it also recognized that to bring some projects to their fullest potential, additional funds were needed.

In 1986 the agency, which the year before had been renamed the New Hampshire State

Council on the Arts, began to seek contributions from sources outside the agency. The first project financed collaboratively was a sculpture for Mount Sunapee State Park. Private agencies (The League of New Hampshire Craftsmen Foundation, Inc., and the Lake Sunapee Business Association) joined with another state agency, the New Hampshire Division of Parks and Recreation, to assume some of the project's costs.

The Council sought an even greater commitment from another state agency when the Arts Center on Brickyard Pond at Keene State College wanted a large-scale stone sculpture for a public entry in the theater complex. The college matched Arts Council funds to commission the artwork. In addition, it paid for shipping the artwork and provided materials and manpower for the installation.

As Percent for Art completes its tenth year, the program's goal of integrating art and architecture has been met with great success in the psychiatric hospital project. With this project, the design of arts spaces and artwork began in the early stages of architectural planning. The artists and architects worked together throughout design and construction phases. Communication among hospital, Arts Council, and project construction administrators grew from awkward encounters into productive, exciting, working relationships.

The participation of so many individuals in the Percent for Art process, once seen as cumbersome, turned out to be one of its greatest strengths. The program will continue to depend on the good will of many, especially the artists, who continue to share their talents with the State of New Hampshire.

The images that follow in this book document the state's permanent collection, art that is in unexpected places, not confined in museum or gallery walls but woven into the fabric of the daily life of New Hampshire's people.

Audrey V. Sylvester
Coordinator, Percent for
Art Program

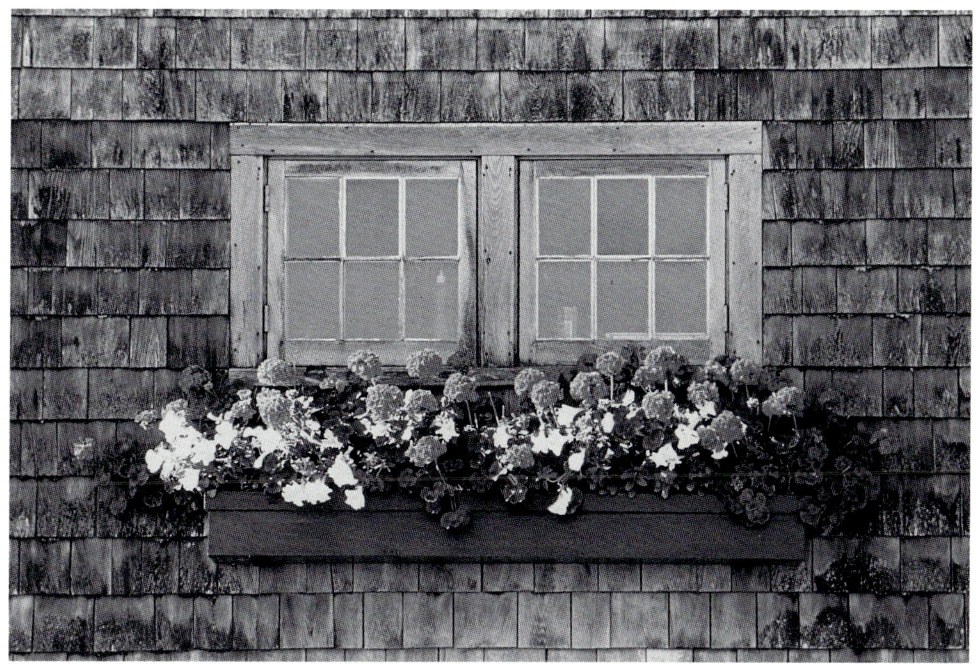

"W I N D O W   B O X"   1 9 7 8

CIBACHROME PHOTOGRAPH
11″ × 14″

A N N E   D U B O I S

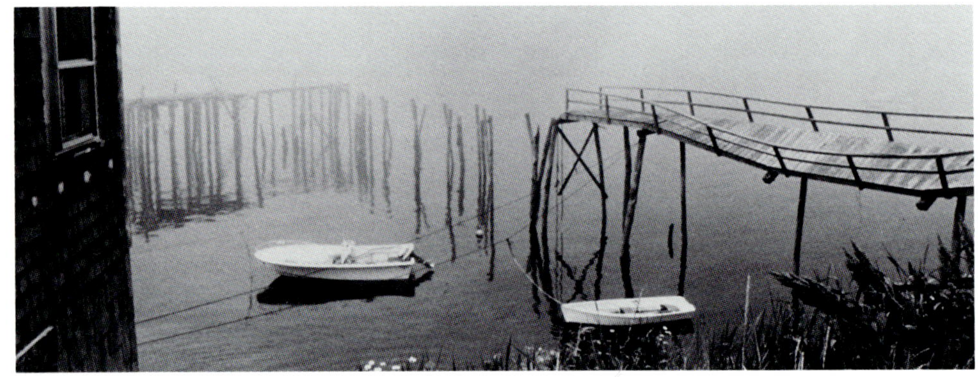

"I N   T H E   C O V E"   1 9 8 4

COLOR PHOTOGRAPH, EKTAFLEX PRINT
$2\frac{1}{2}$" × $6\frac{1}{2}$"

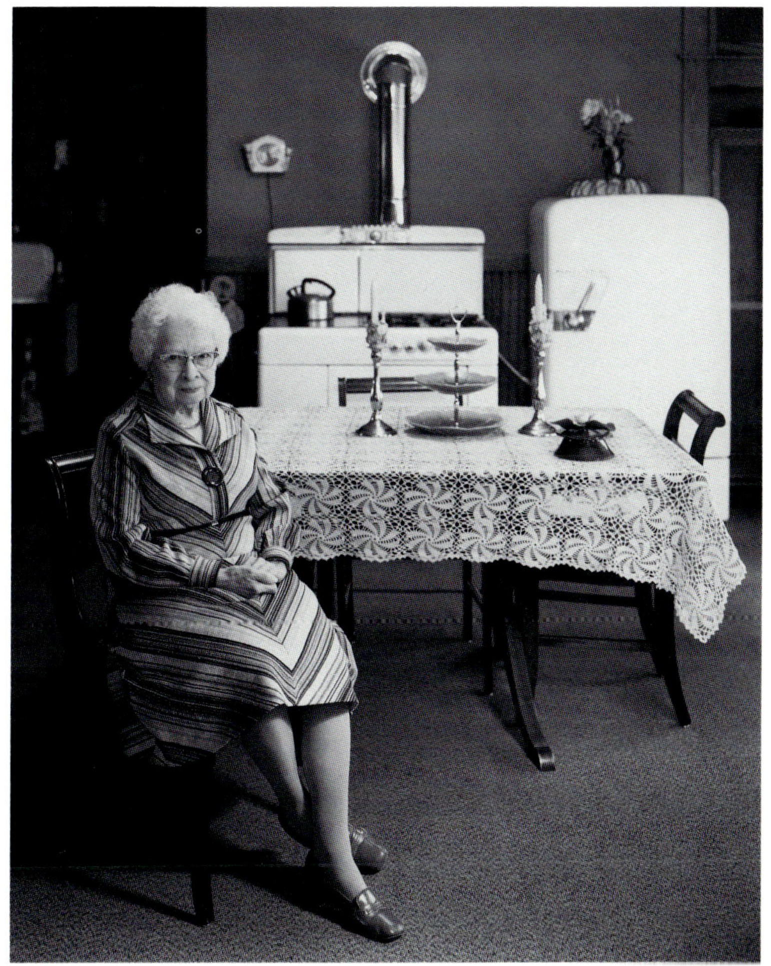

"VIOLETTE LECLERC AT 321 CARTIER ST.,
MANCHESTER, NH" 1983

BLACK AND WHITE PHOTOGRAPH
9" × 7"

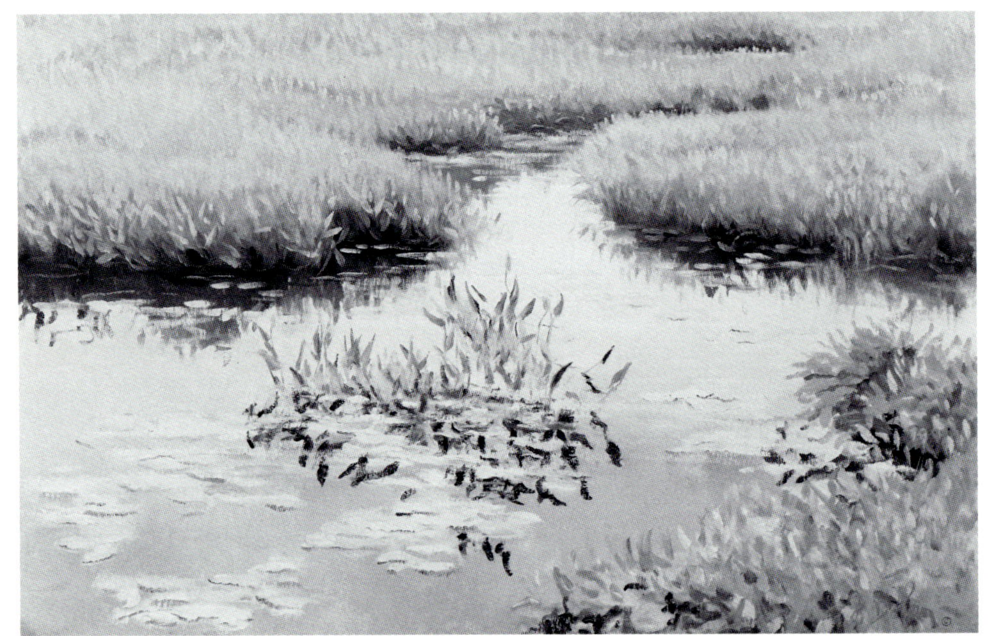

"FLOWERING MARSH" 1981

OIL ON CANVAS
24″ × 30″

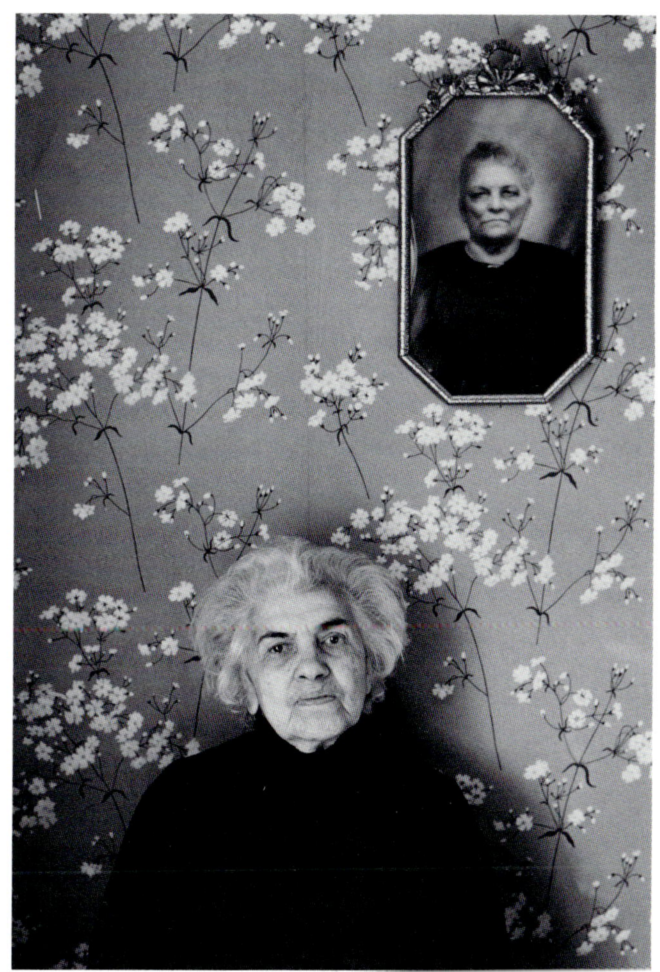

"H E L E N   P R A E T E"   1 9 7 9

CIBACHROME PHOTOGRAPH
9½″ × 6½″

ERIC F. SINCLAIR

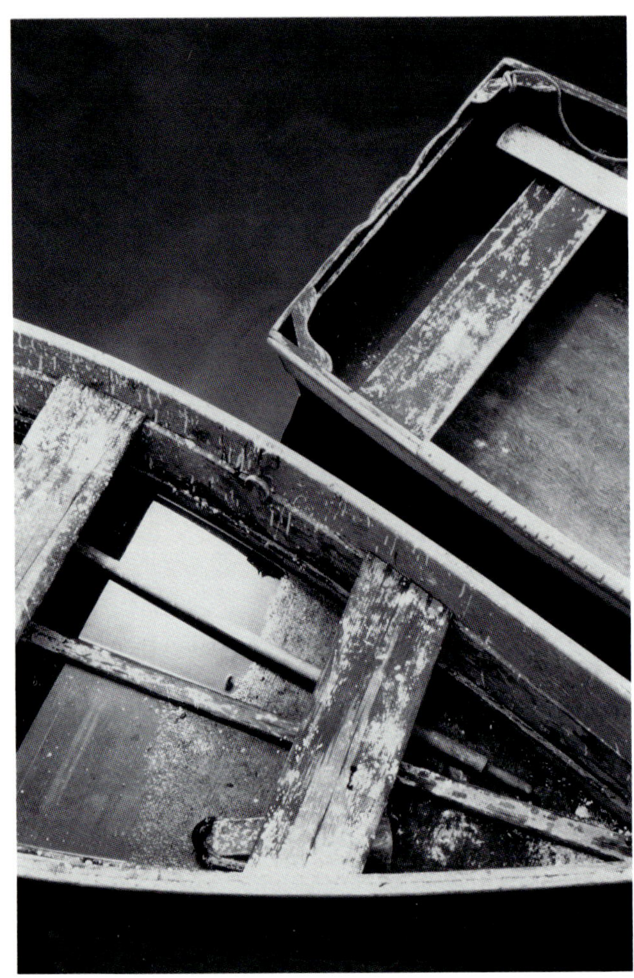

"TWO BOATS" 1970

CIBACHROME PHOTOGRAPH
$6\frac{3}{8}'' \times 9\frac{5}{16}''$

ELEANOR BRIGGS

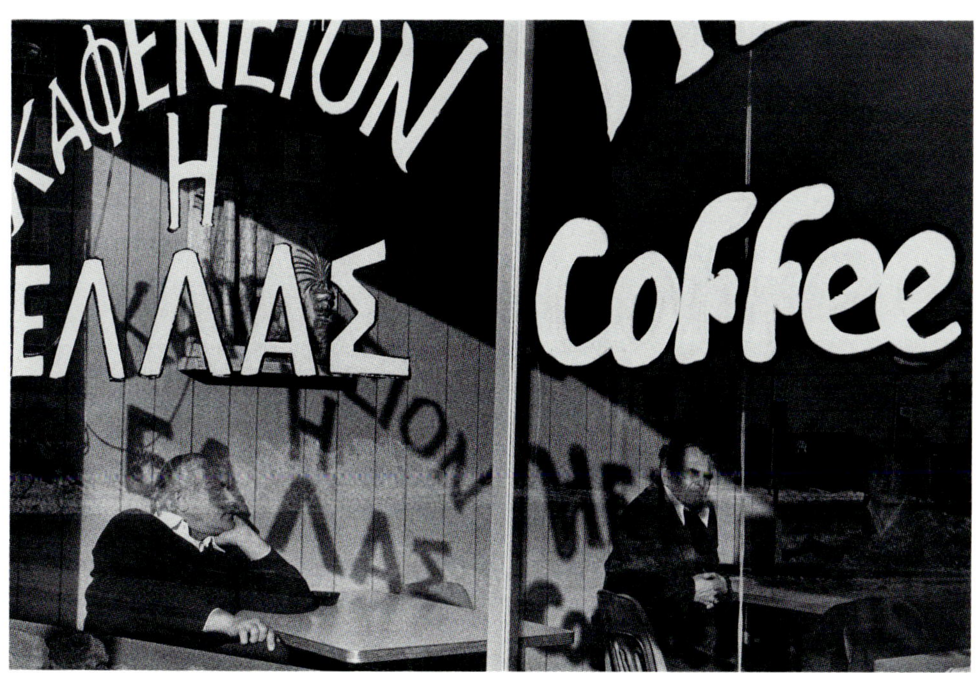

"PORTRAIT OF MANCHESTER" 1982

BLACK AND WHITE PHOTOGRAPH
11″ × 14″

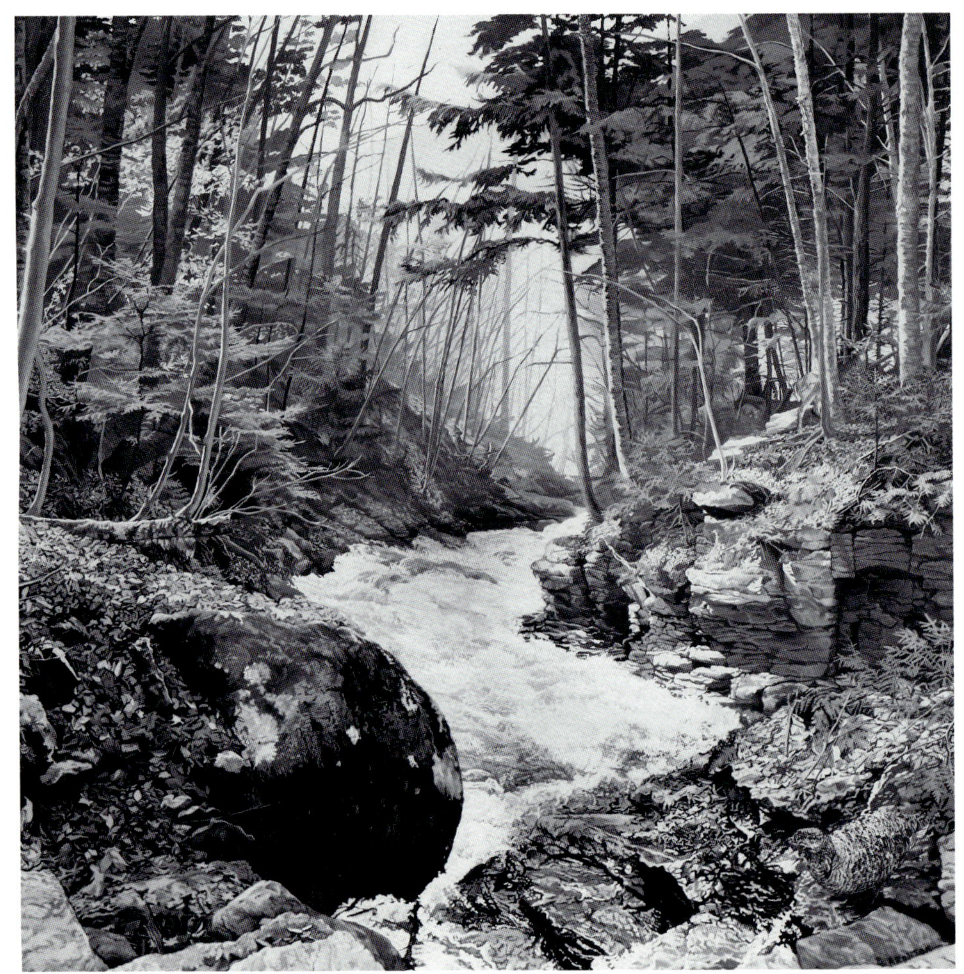

"C A S C A D I N G   W O O D L A N D   S T R E A M"   1 9 8 8

OIL ON CANVAS
6′ × 6′

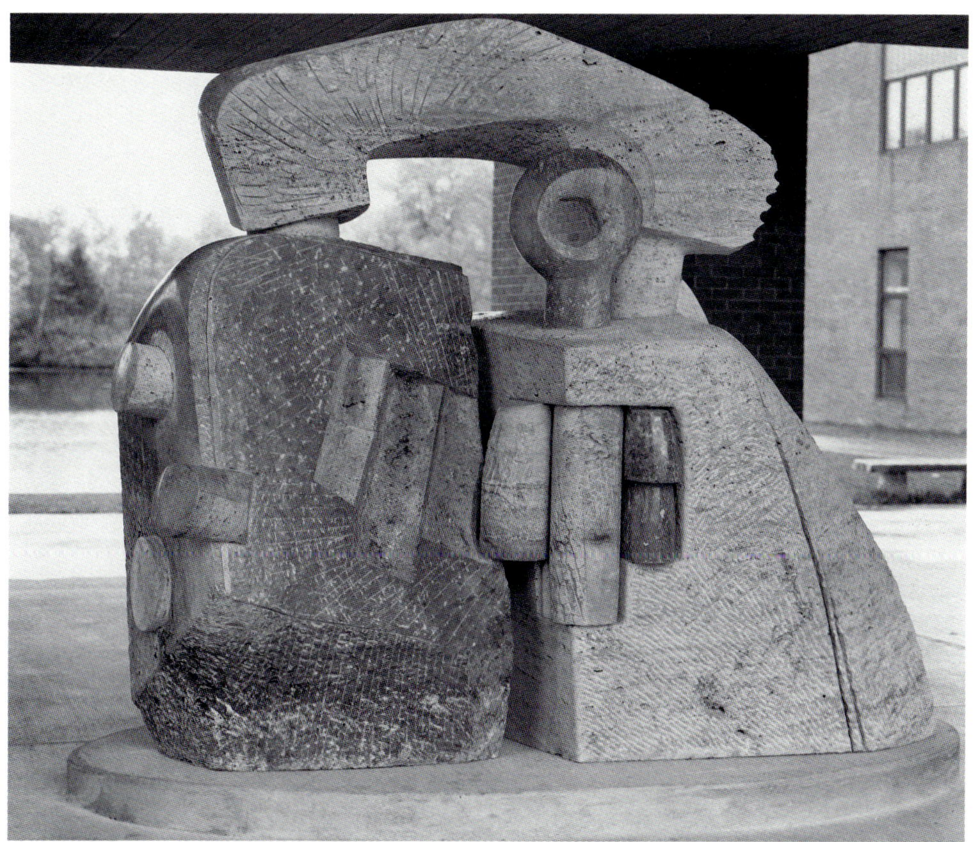

"ATHANOR" 1988

ITALIAN TRAVERTINE
7' × 9' × 4'

JULIE S. SERRANO

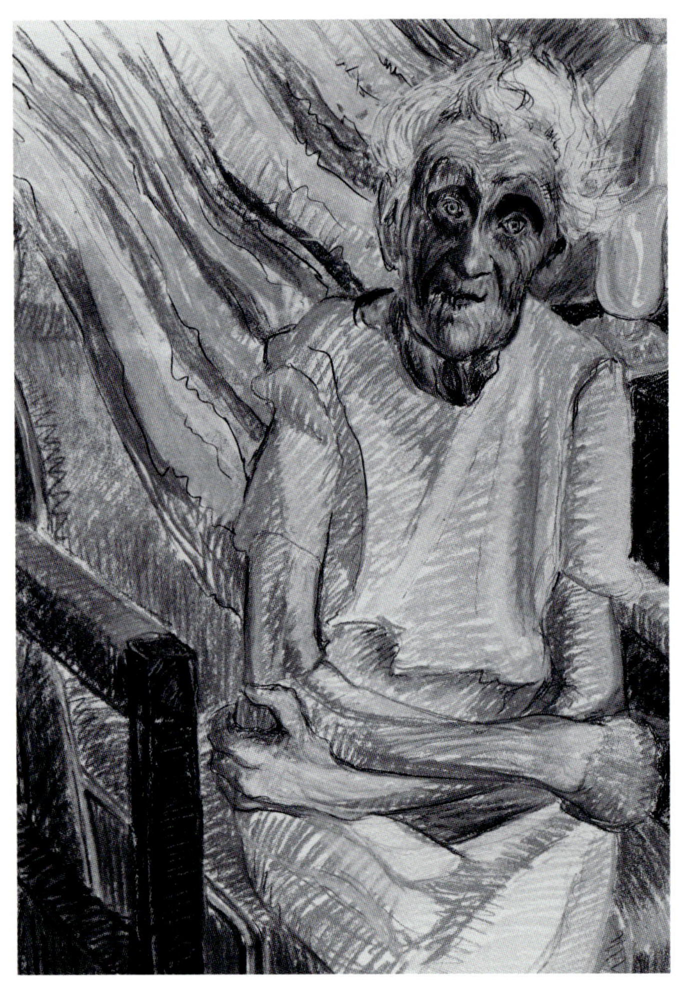

"HANNA" 1980

PASTEL AND PENCIL
37″ × 28″

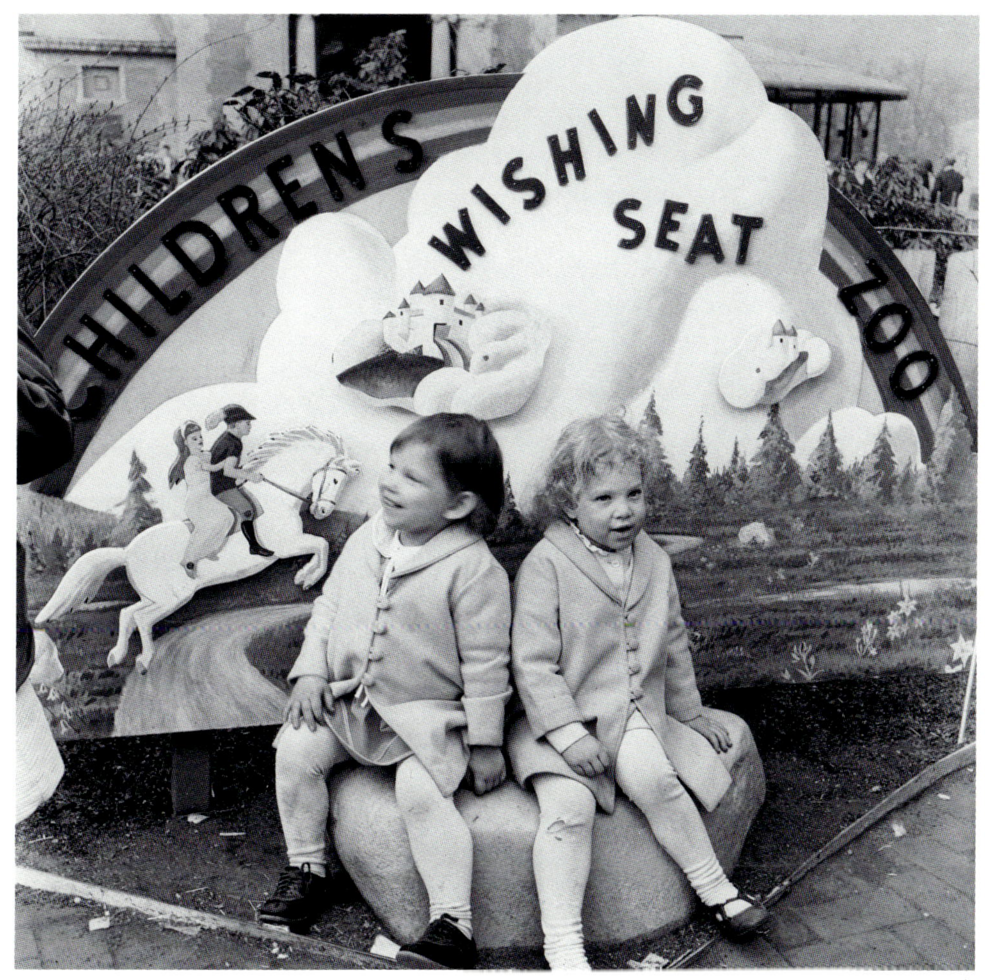

"THE WISHING SEAT" 1981

OIL COLOR OVER COLOR PHOTOGRAPH
23″ × 21″

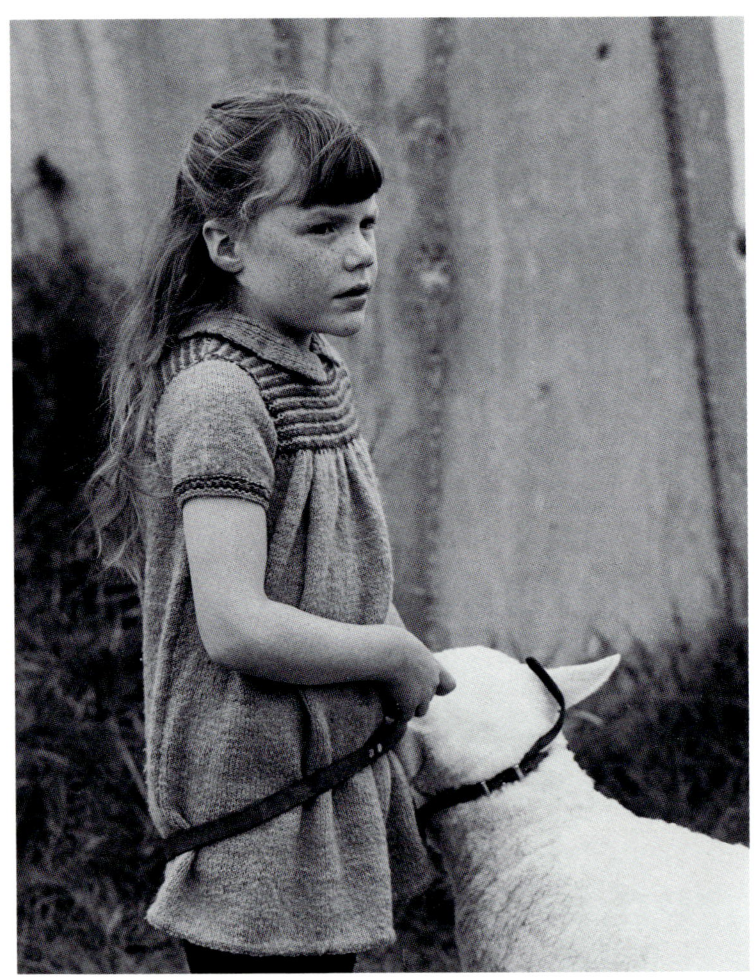

"COUNTRY FAIR, CORNISH, NEW HAMPSHIRE" 1982

BLACK AND WHITE PHOTOGRAPH
10″ × 8″

N O R M A N   F R A N C O E U R

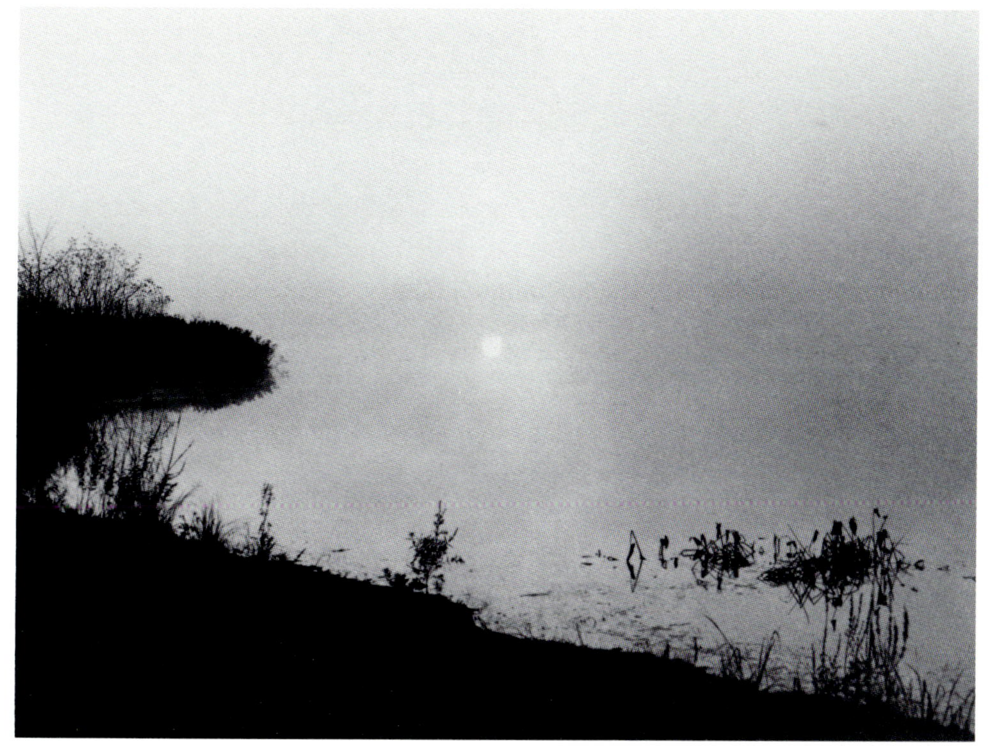

" W A T E R   A N D   R E E D S "   1 9 8 5

TYPE C COLOR PHOTOGRAPH
11″ × 14″

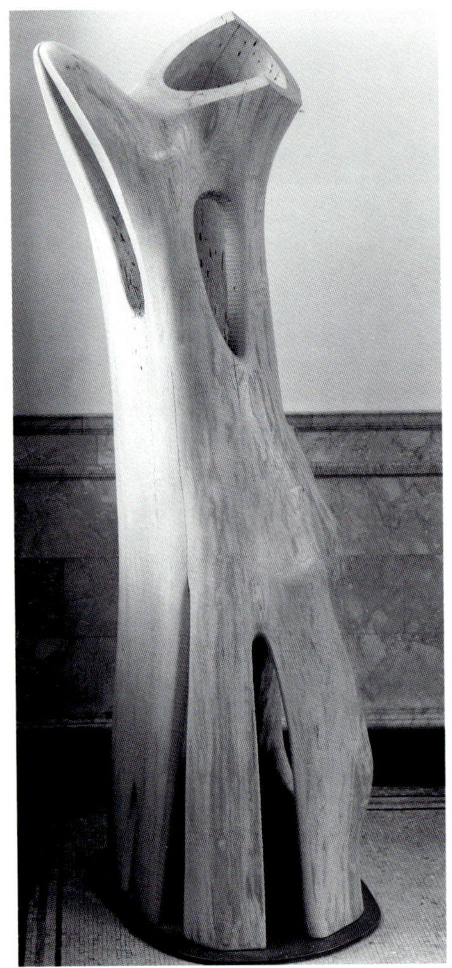

"T H E   B E R R Y   E L M   S C U L P T U R E"   1 9 8 3 - 8 4

ELM WOOD
10′ × 3′ × 3′

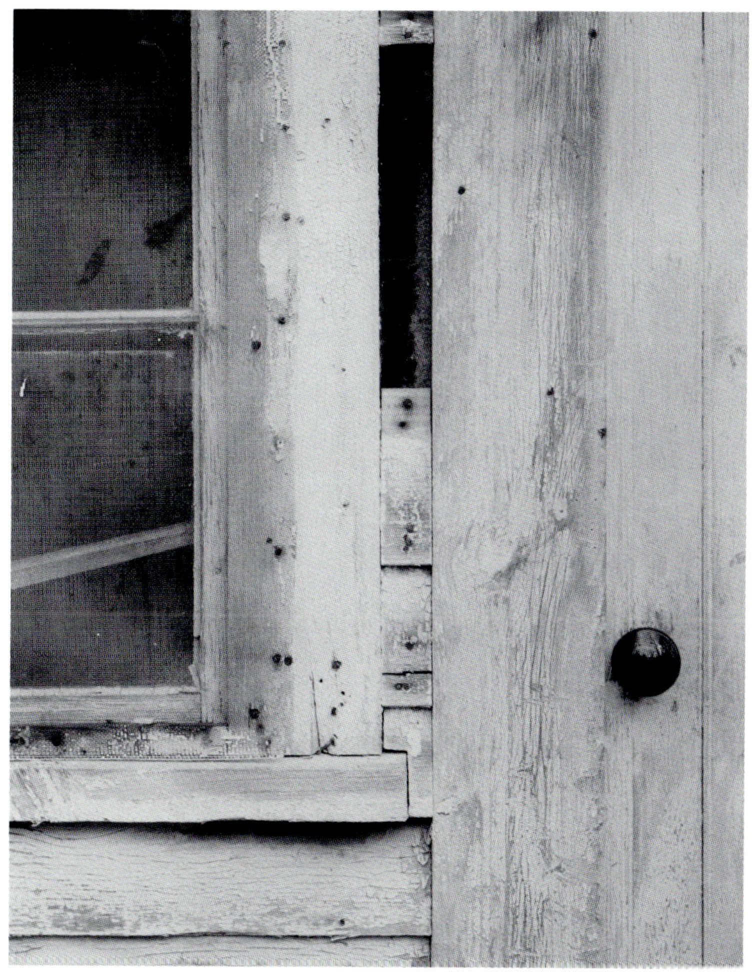

"PORCELAIN DOORKNOB" 1983

CIBACHROME PHOTOGRAPH
8″ × 10″

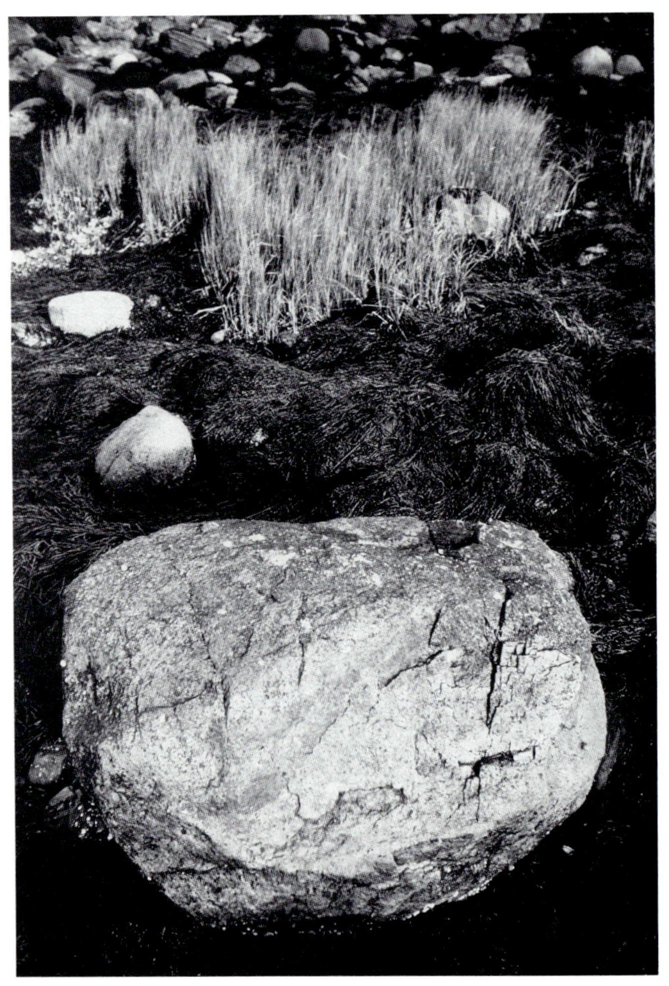

"R O C K   A N D   E E L   G R A S S ,   F A L L"   1 9 7 5

CIBACHROME PHOTOGRAPH
24" × 20"

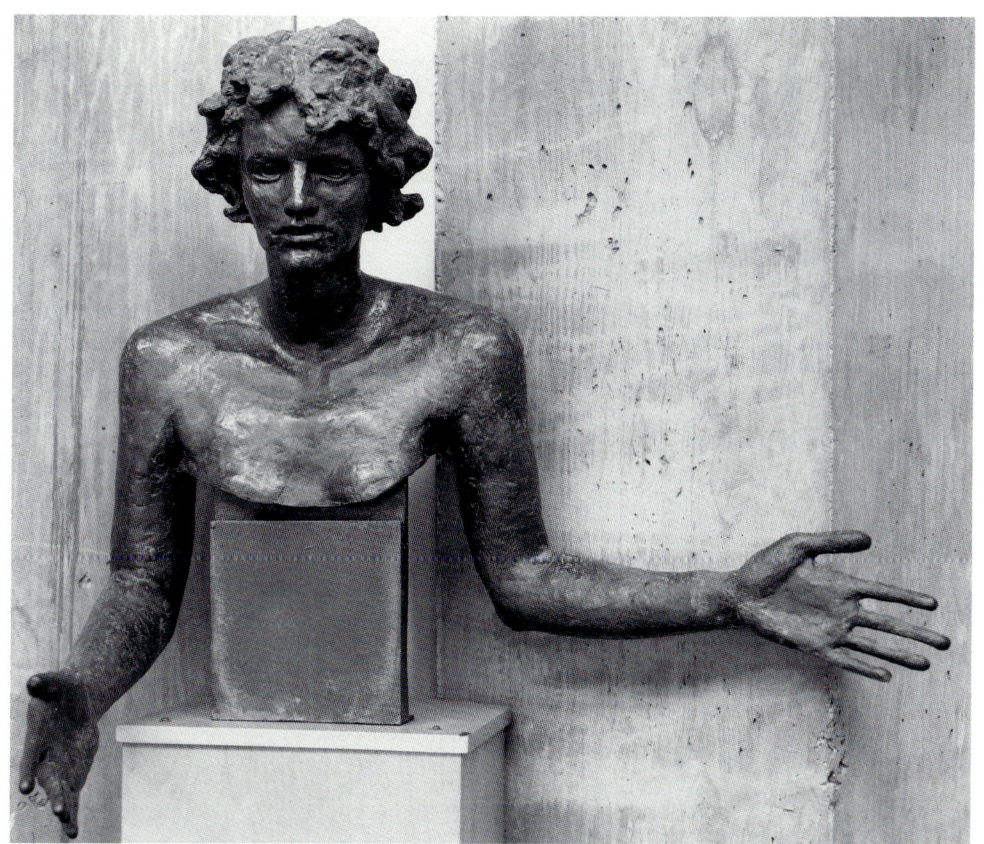

"TRIPTYCH" 1983

BRONZE
28" × 37" × 24"

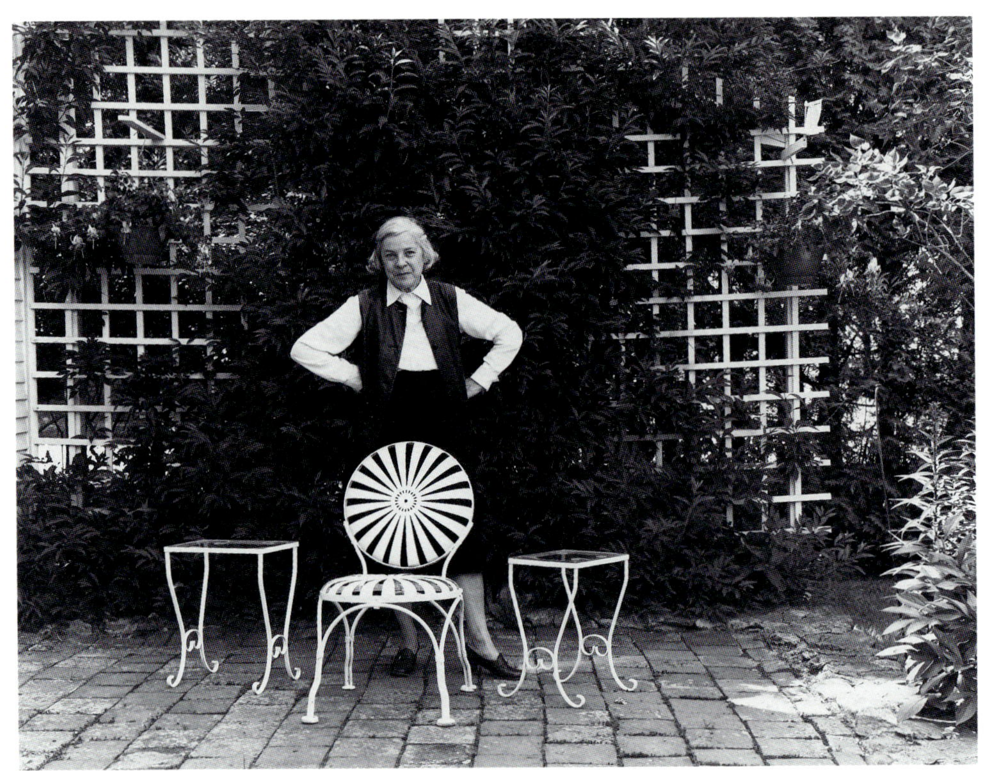

"PORTRAIT OF MARY MCCARTHY" 1981

BLACK AND WHITE PHOTOGRAPH
8″ × 10″

A D R I E N N E   C A M P B E L L

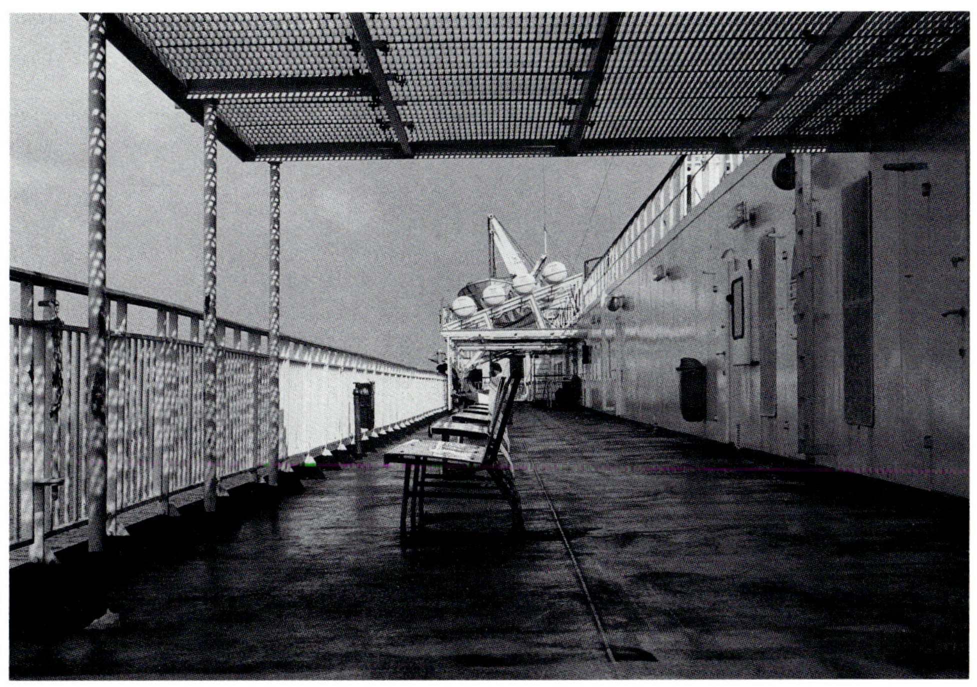

"S T E A M E R - S T O C K H O L M - T U R K U"   1 9 8 2

BLACK AND WHITE PHOTOGRAPH
$6^{13}/_{16}$" × $10^{3}/_{16}$"

JOHN W. HATCH

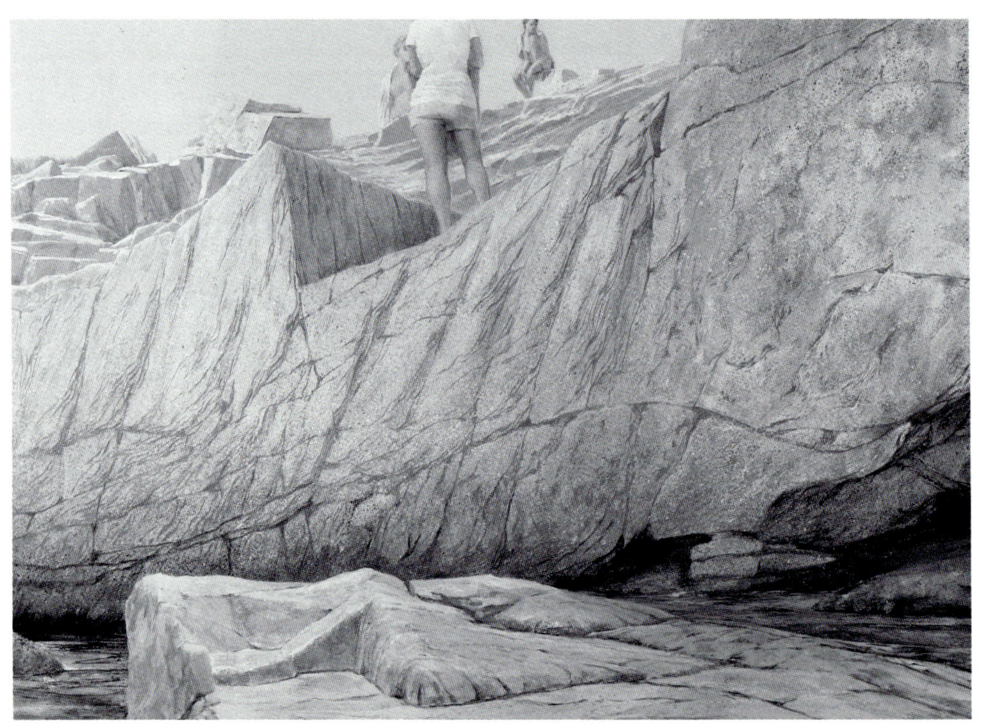

"CELIA'S ISLAND (ISLES OF SHOALS—
APPLEDORE ISLAND)" 1978

ACRYLIC ON MASONITE
36″ × 48″

P A U L   S .   H O W E

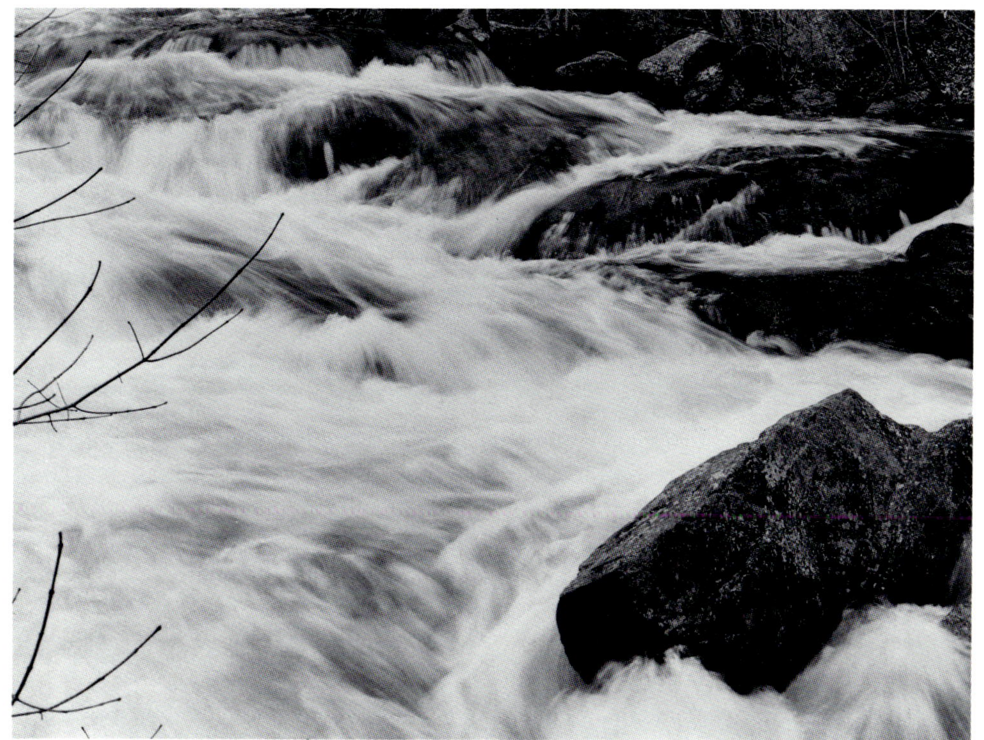

"K I M P T O N   B R O O K   I I I"   1 9 8 4

BLACK AND WHITE PHOTOGRAPH
11″ × 14″

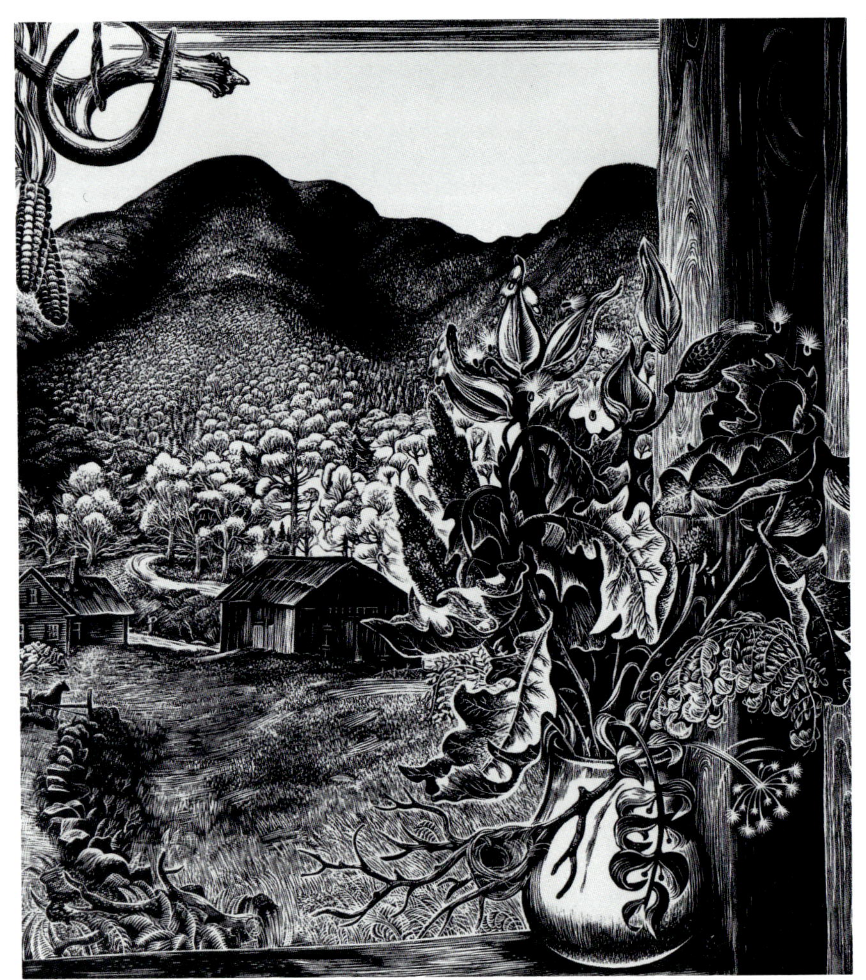

"A U T U M N   B O U Q U E T"   1 9 7 9

WOOD ENGRAVING
$7\frac{1}{2}$" × $6\frac{5}{8}$"

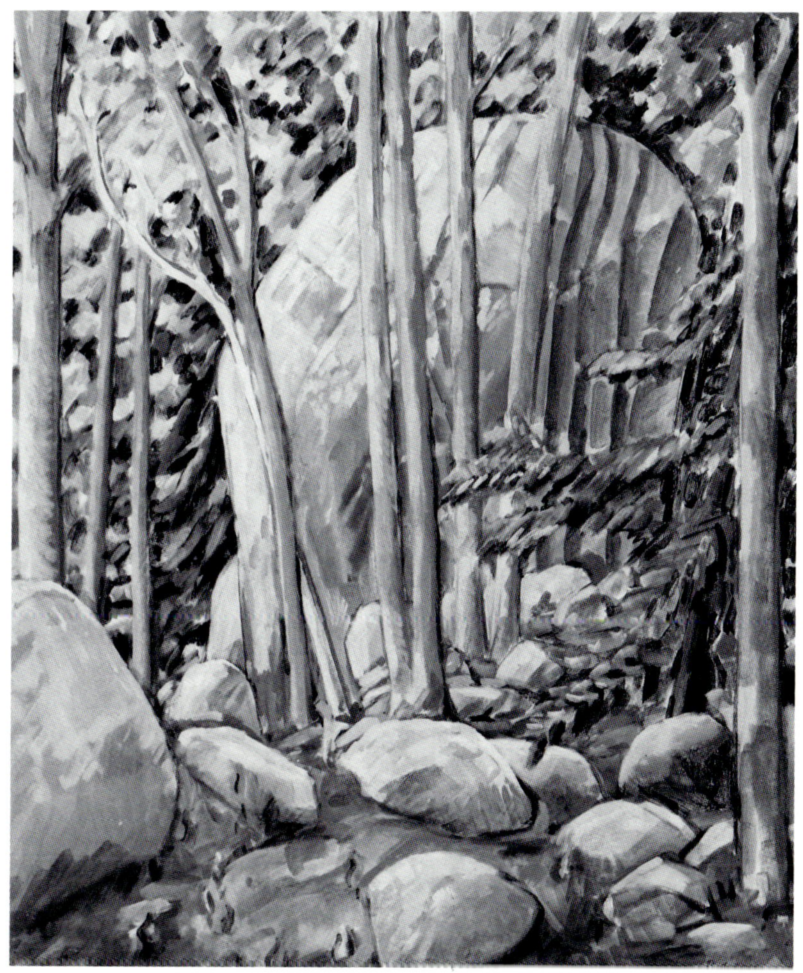

"BOULDER" 1979

ACRYLIC ON CANVAS
35" × 29"

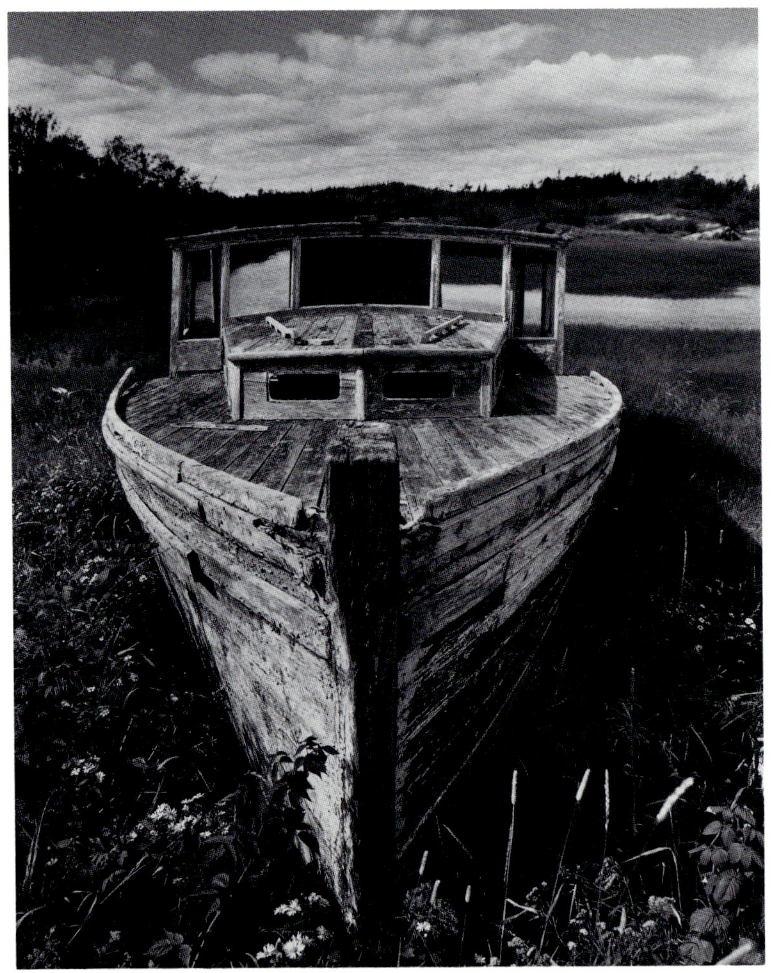

"T H E   O L D   B O A T"   1 9 7 9

CIBACHROME PHOTOGRAPH
11″ × 14″

"A U T U M N   L A N D S C A P E"   1 9 8 0

SERIGRAPH–ARTIST'S PROOF
28″ × 20″

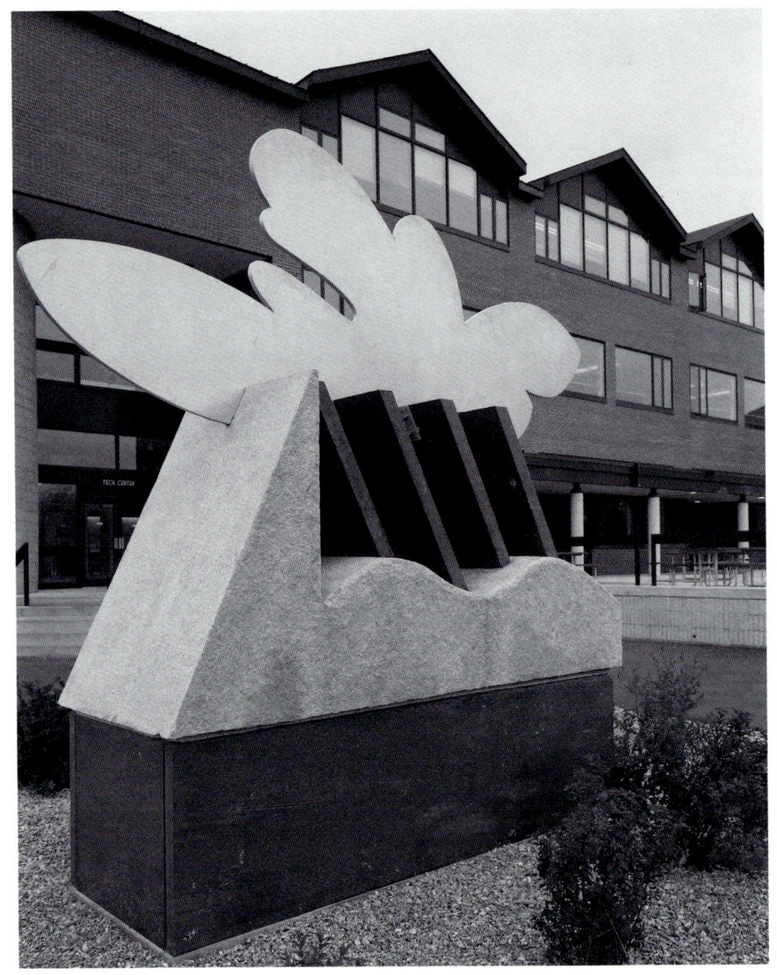

"T H E   C R O S S I N G"   1 9 8 4 - 8 5

BLACK AUSTRALIAN AND GREY CONCORD GRANITE, ALUMINUM
88″ × 120″ × 36″

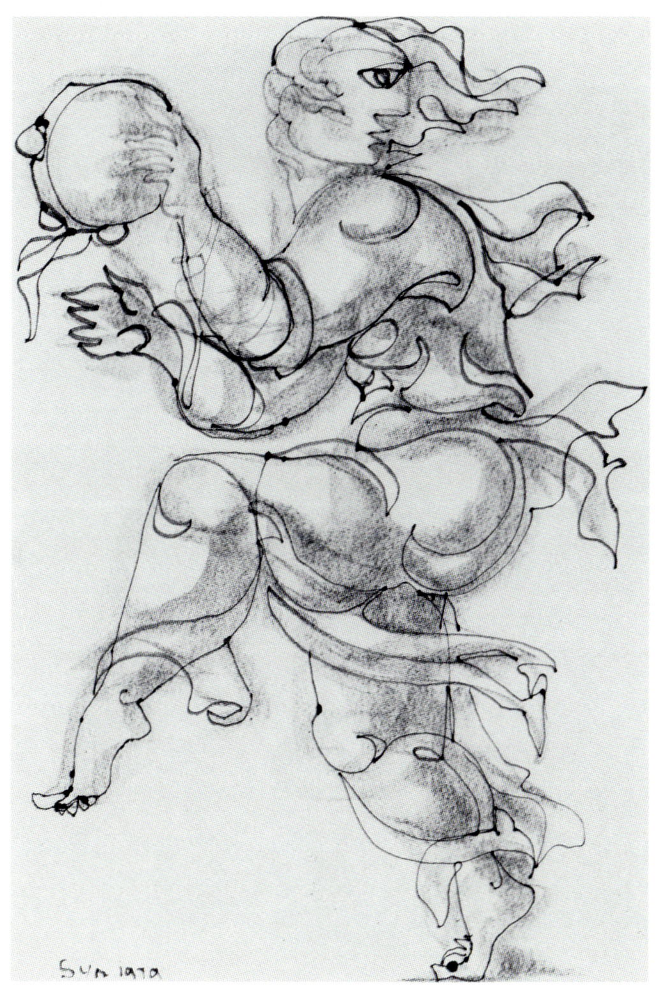

"T H E   D A N C E R"   1 9 7 9

CONTE CRAYON AND INK
24½" × 18"

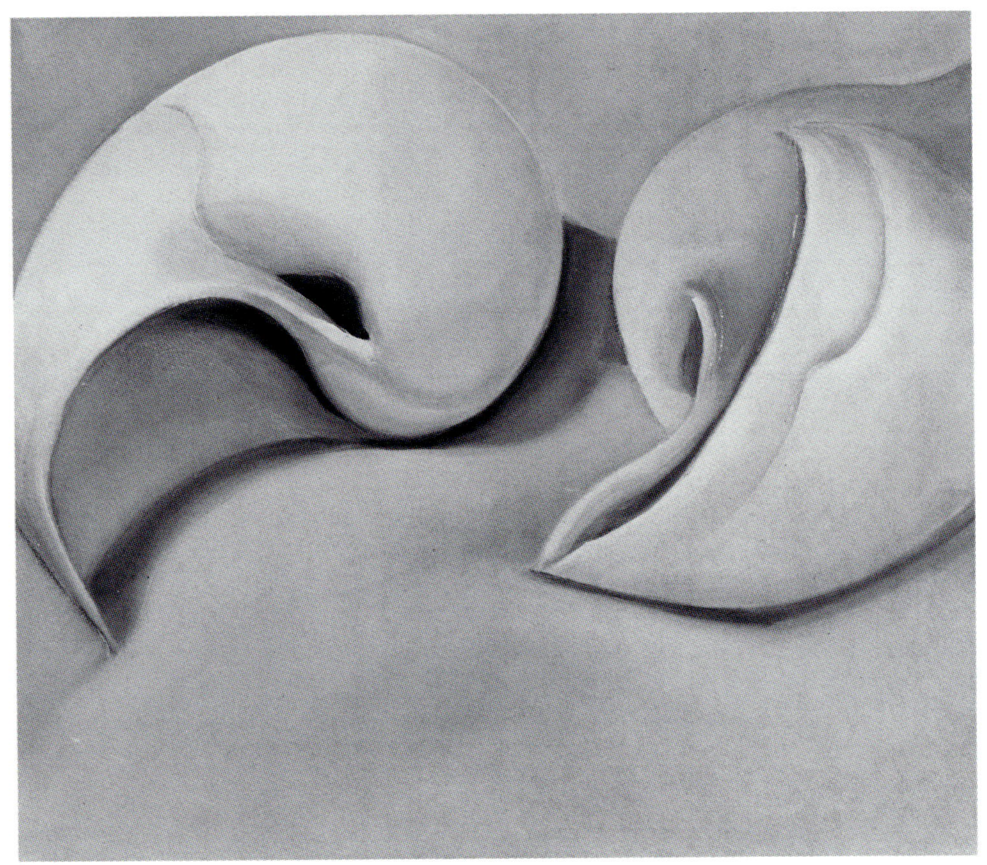

"M O O N   S H E L L S"   1 9 8 4

OIL ON LINEN
$12\frac{3}{4}'' \times 15\frac{5}{16}''$

S U S A N   D .   H O W E

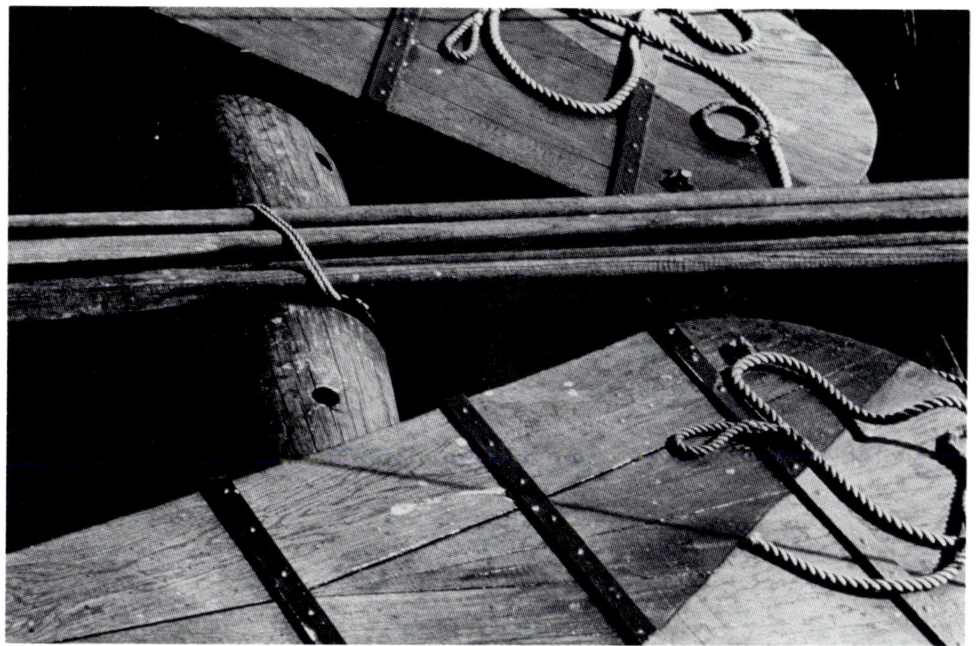

"O A R S   A N D   R O P E S"   1 9 8 2

CIBACHROME PHOTOGRAPH
8" × 12"

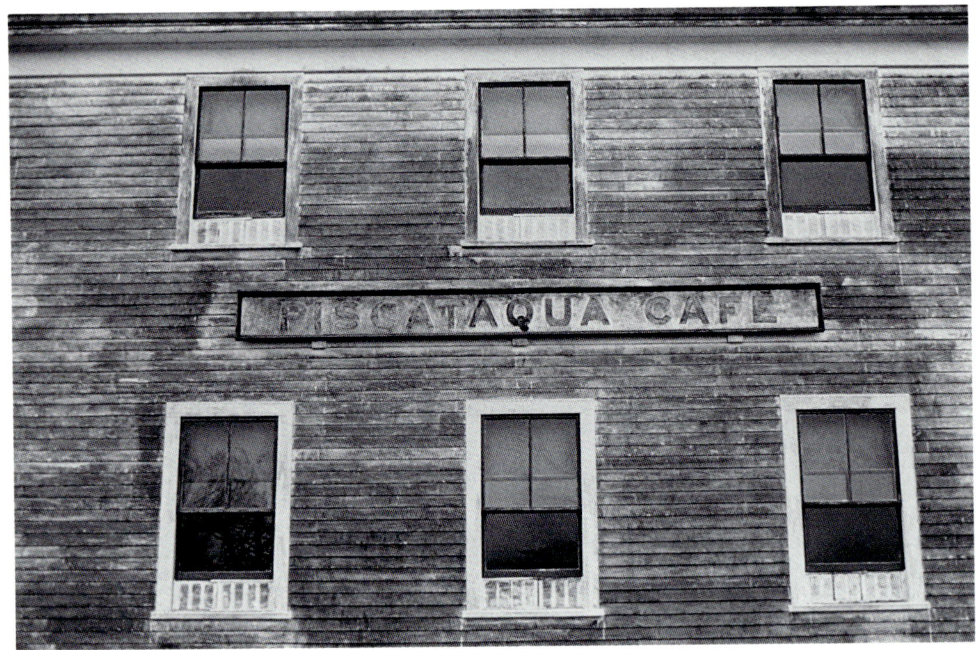

"P I S C A T A Q U A   C A F E"   1 9 7 8

CIBACHROME PHOTOGRAPH
10″ × 14″

R I C H A R D   T .   S L A T E R

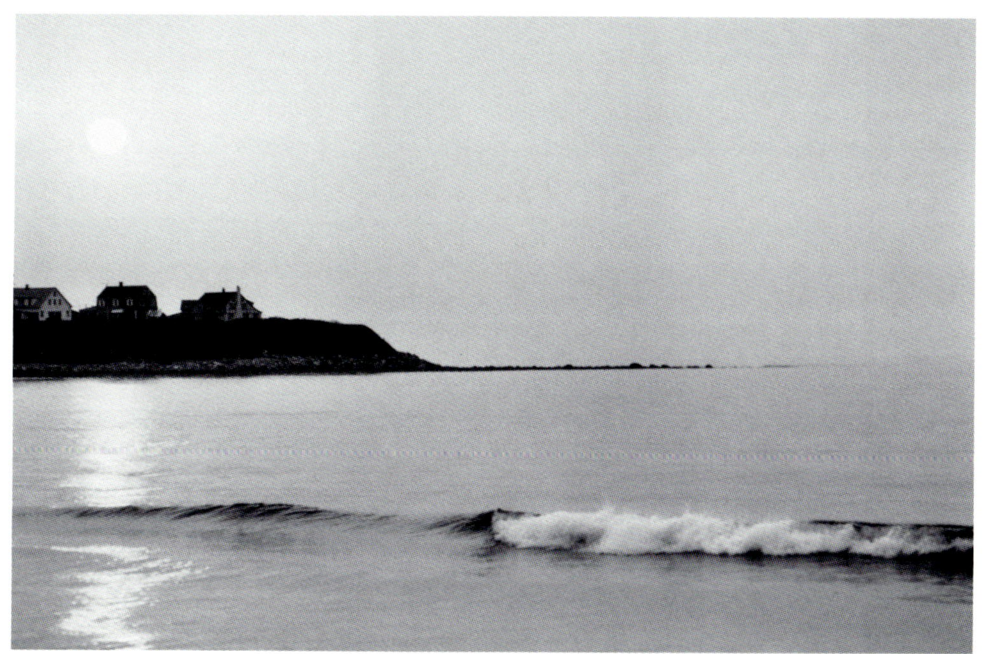

"H A M P T O N   B E A C H ,   S U N R I S E" 1 9 8 0

CIBACHROME PHOTOGRAPH
11″ × 14″

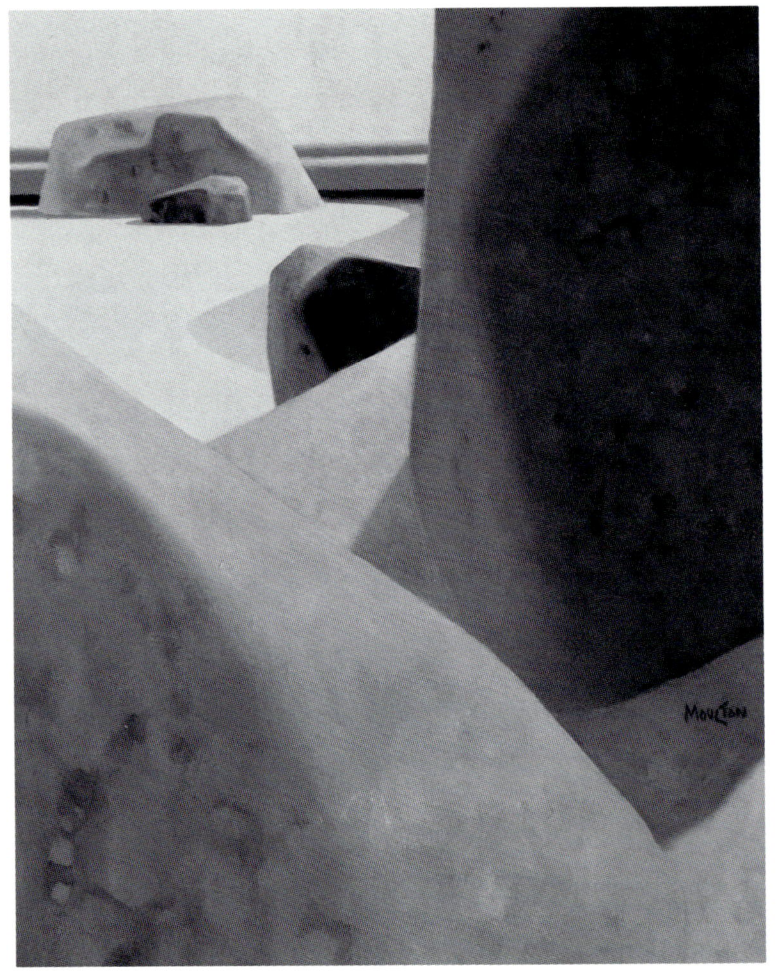

" Q U I N T E T "   1 9 8 2

OIL ON CANVAS BOARD
30″ × 24″

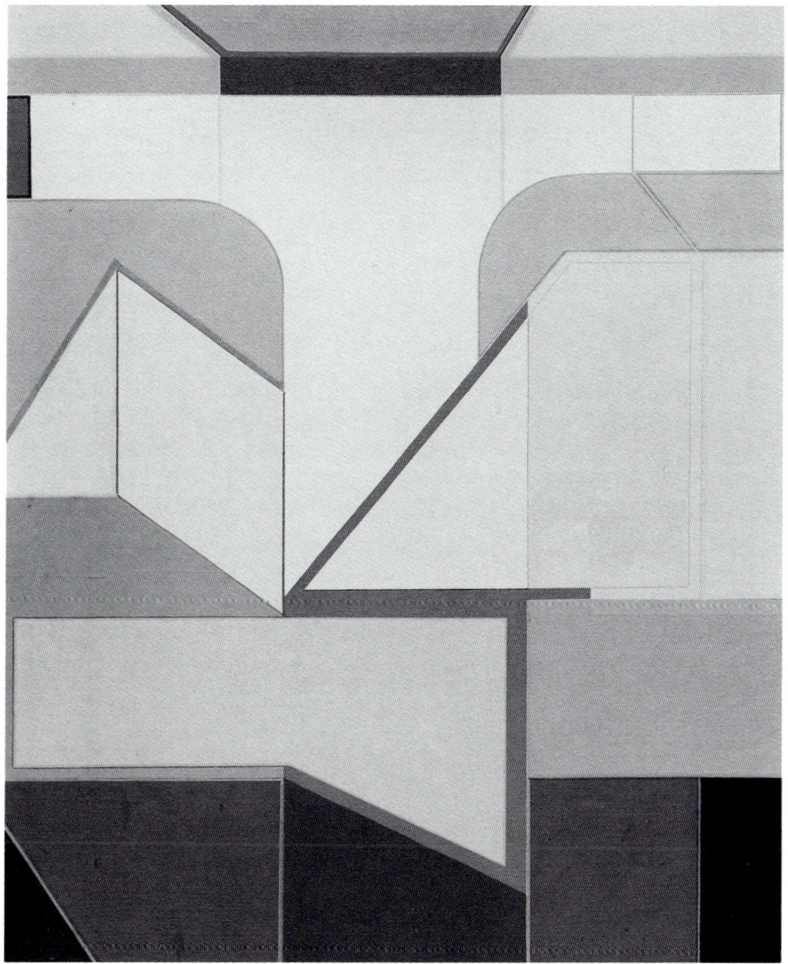

"B R I D G E   # 1 1 2"   1 9 8 2

OIL ON COTTON
60" × 48"

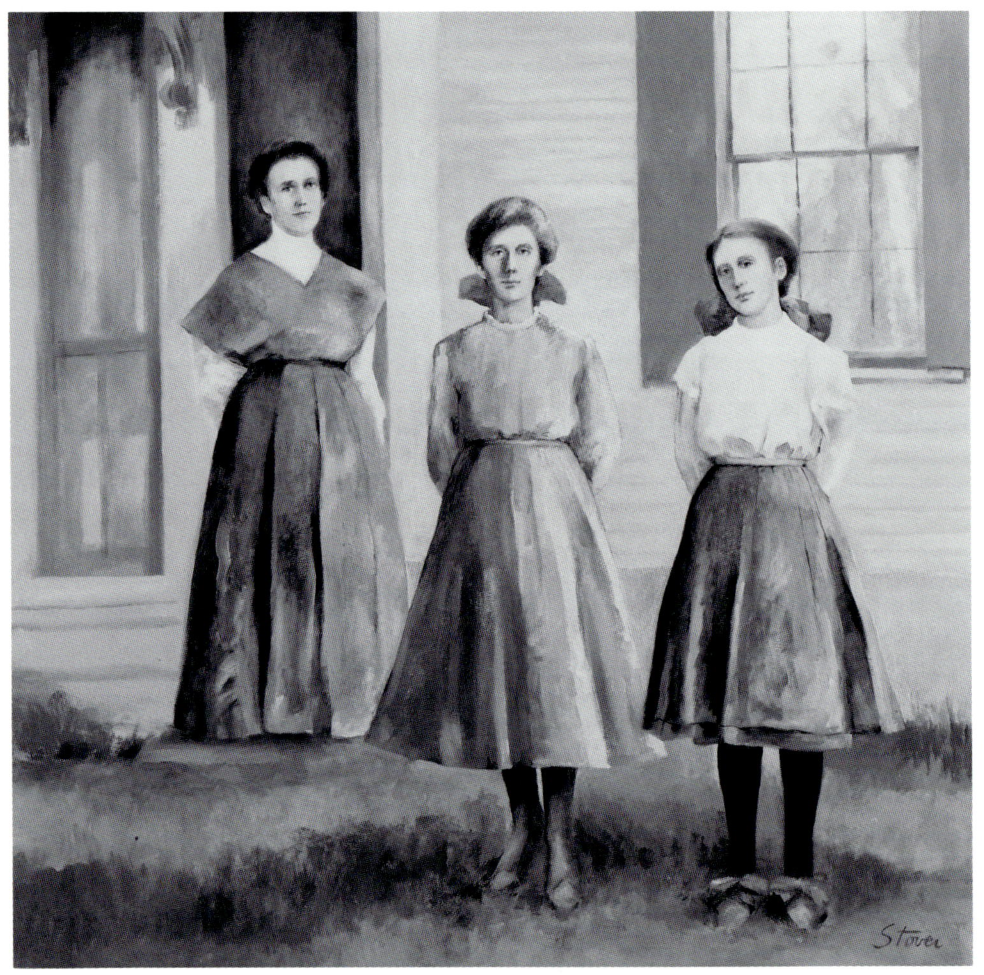

"T H R E E   S I S T E R S"   1 9 8 0

OIL ON COTTON
30" × 30"

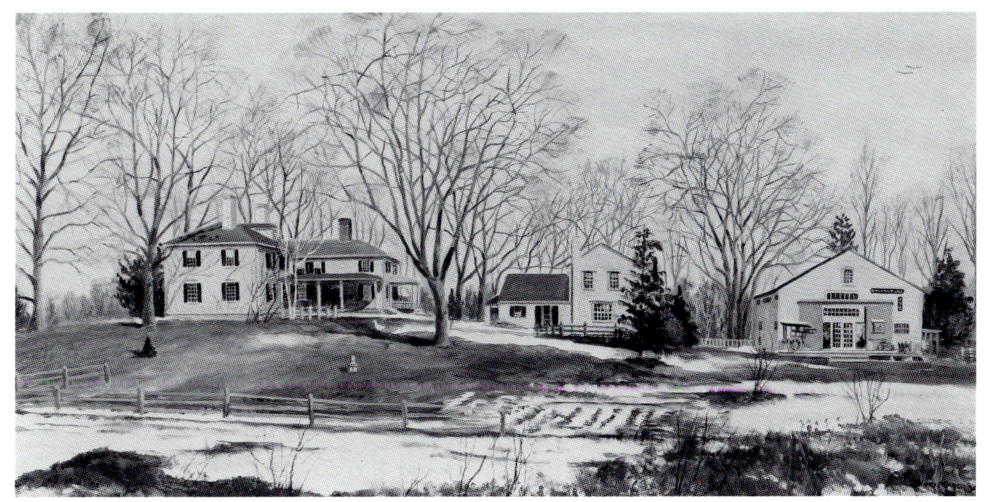

"T H E   C O L L E C T O R ' S   E Y E"   1 9 8 4

OIL ON CANVAS
38″ × 20″

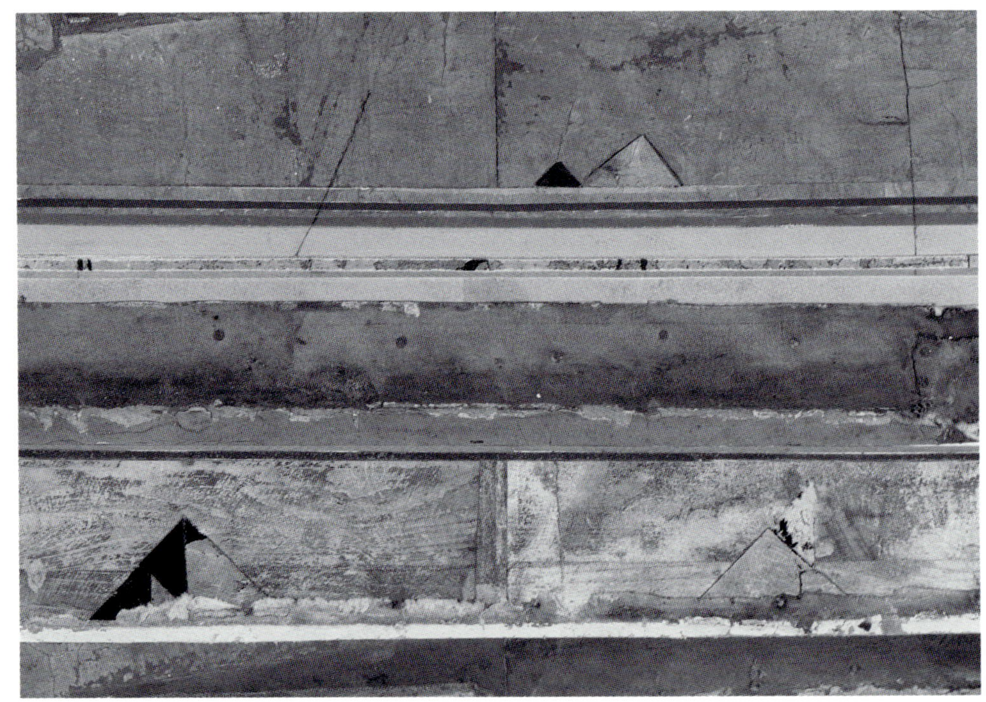

" P Y R A M I D A L "   1 9 8 2

OIL COLLAGE PAINTING
20½" × 26"

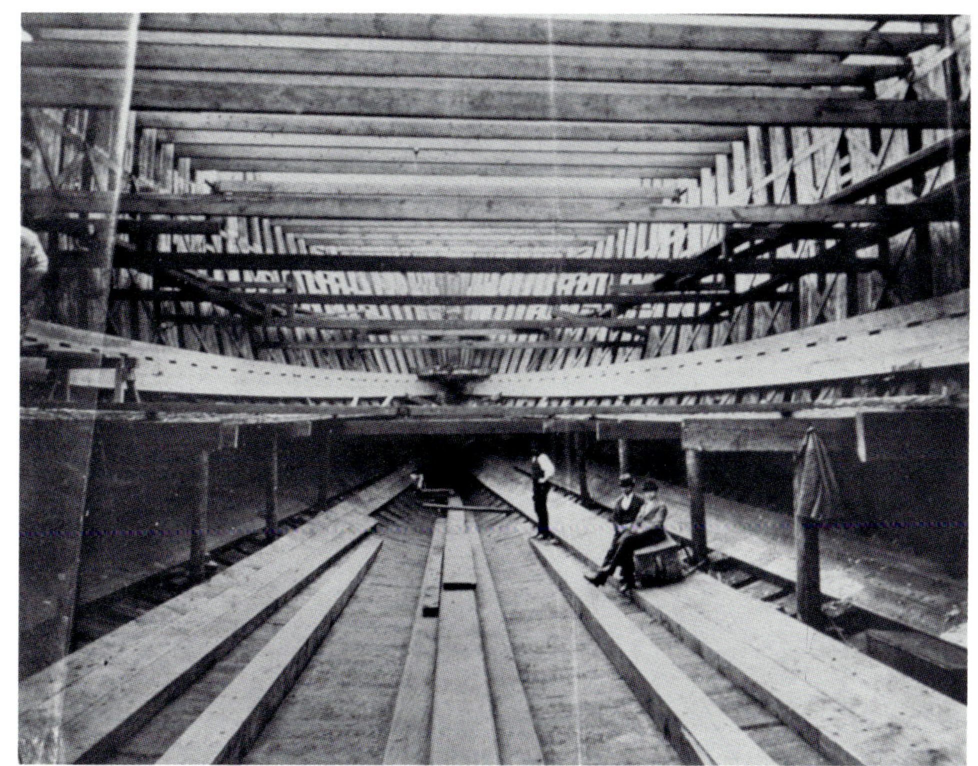

"BELOW DECK CONSTRUCTION, MAN-OF-WAR,
PORTSMOUTH NAVAL SHIPYARD" CIRCA 1880

FROM THE SOUTH BERWICK HISTORICAL
SOCIETY'S COLLECTION

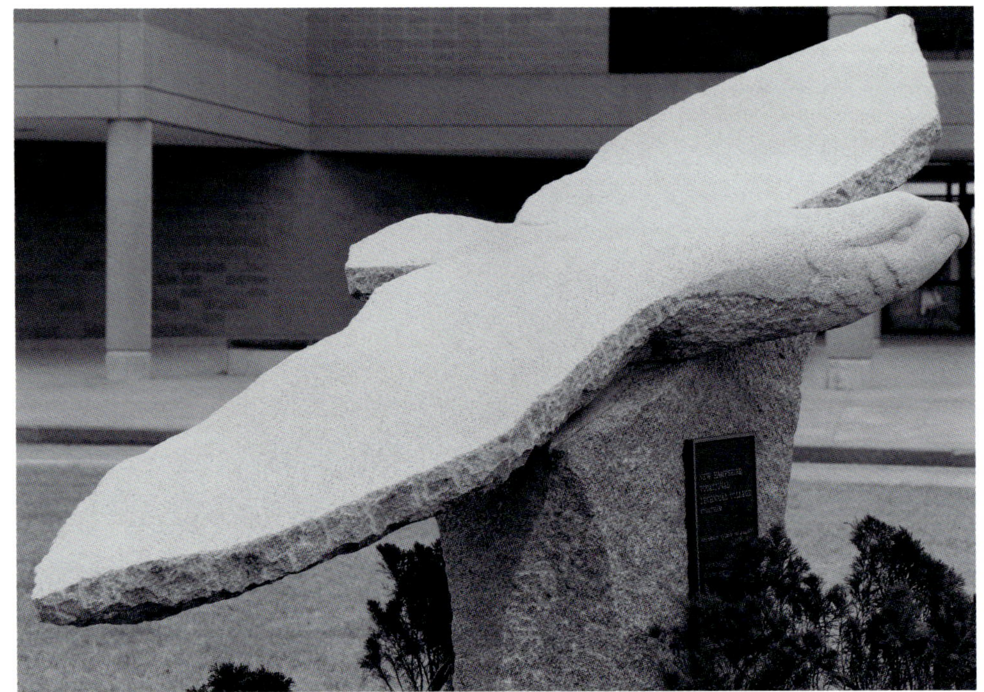

"S E A   B I R D"   1 9 8 4

GRANITE
7′ × 12′ × 5′

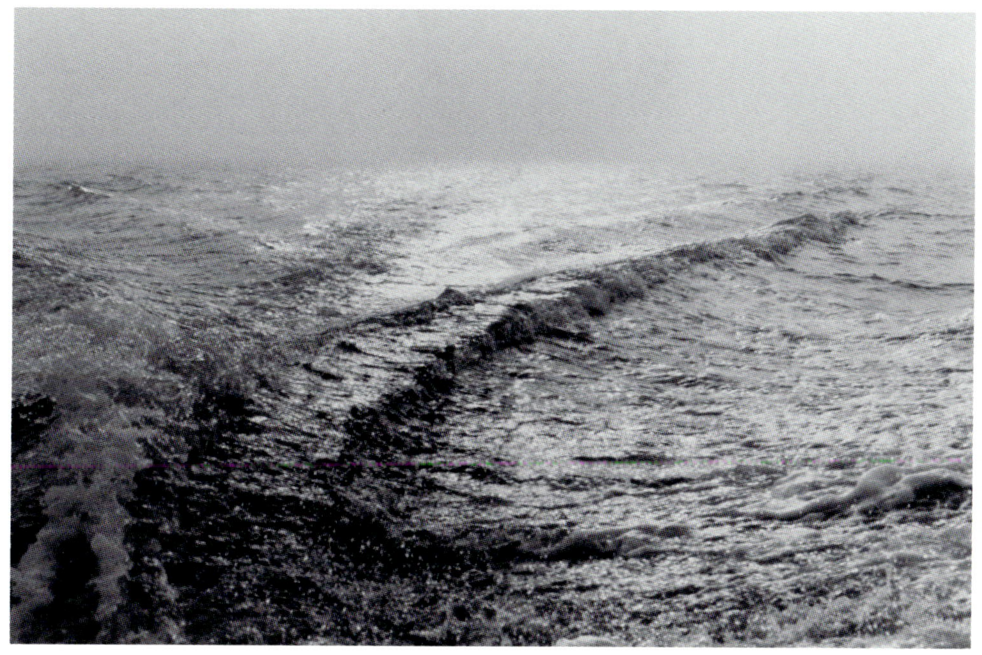

"EARLY MORNING" 1981

TYPE C COLOR PHOTOGRAPH
8″ × 10″

S. C. VALESTRO

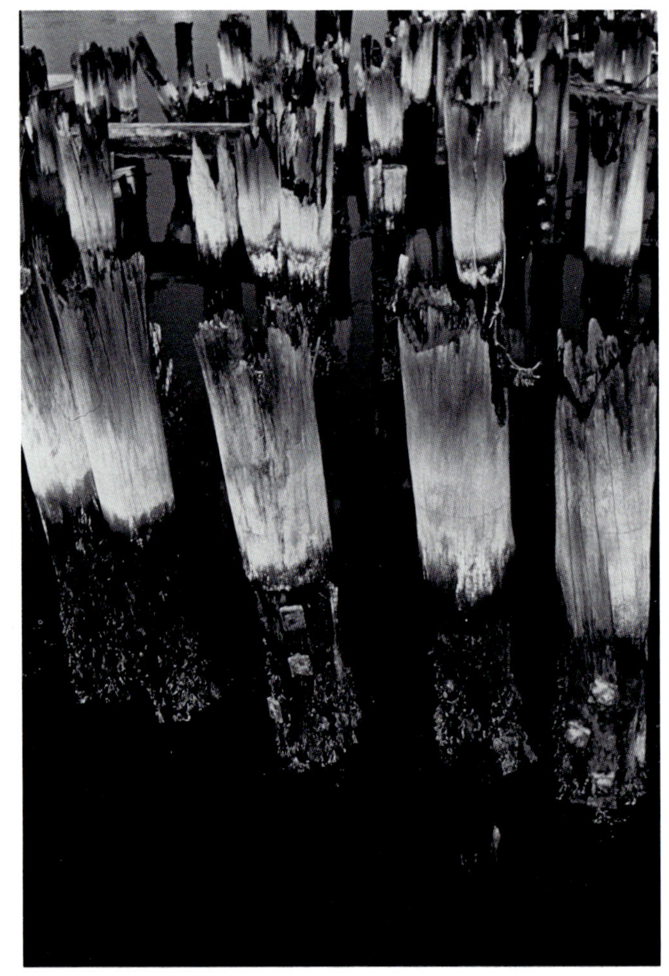

"PILINGS AT VIKING DOCK,
PORTSMOUTH, NEW HAMPSHIRE" 1978

TYPE C COLOR PHOTOGRAPH
13" × 9"

I R E N E E . D U P O N T

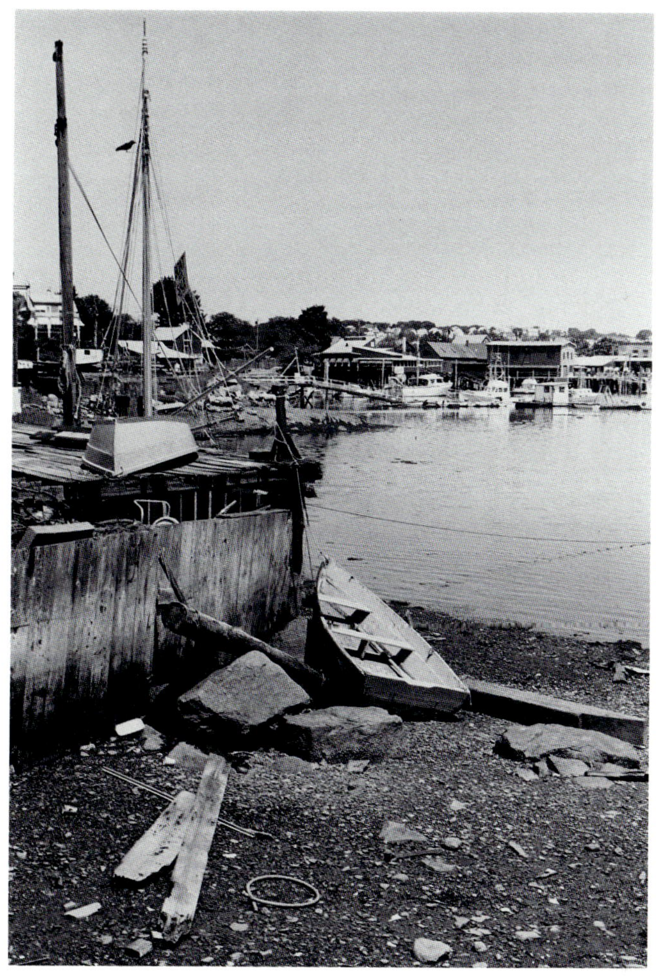

"T I D E ' S O U T" 1 9 8 4

HAND-COLORED PHOTOGRAPH, VANDYKE PROCESS
7″ × 10″

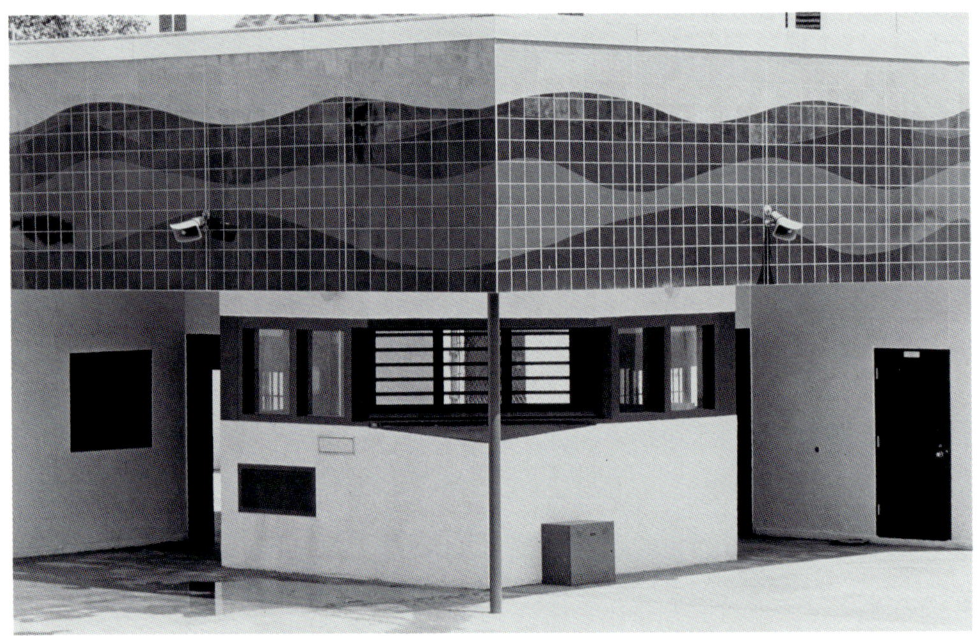

"L A N D S C A P E   M U R A L"   1 9 8 5

HANDPAINTED QUARRY TILES
$9' \times 65' \times \frac{1}{2}''$

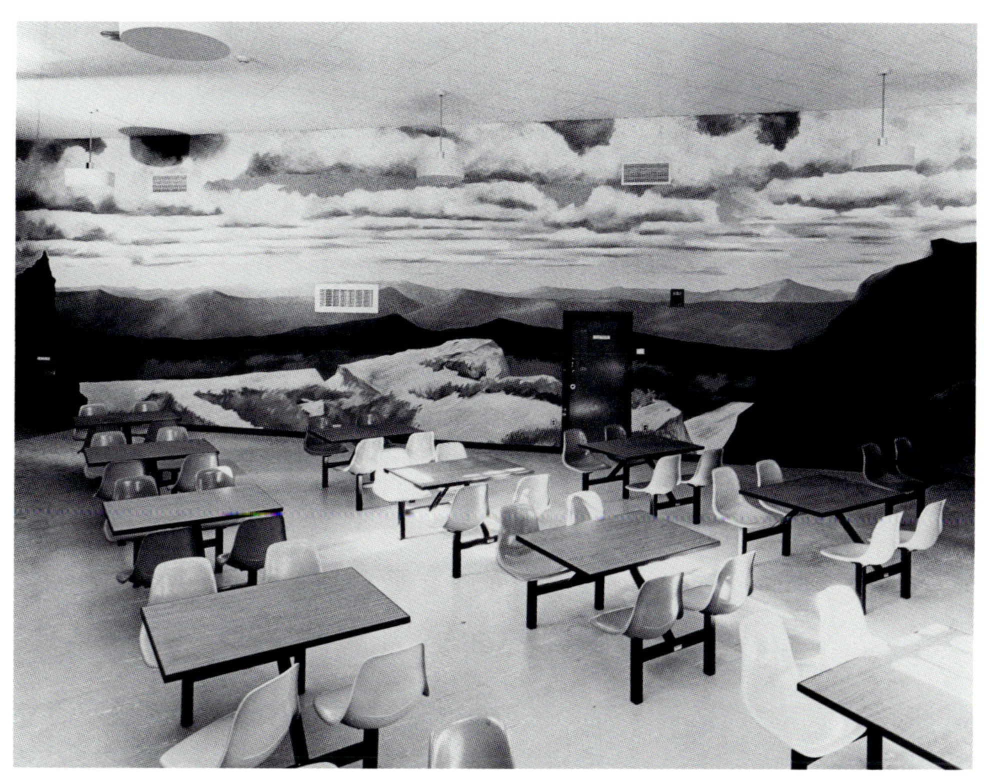

ACRYLIC ON CEMENT BLOCK
16′ × 48′

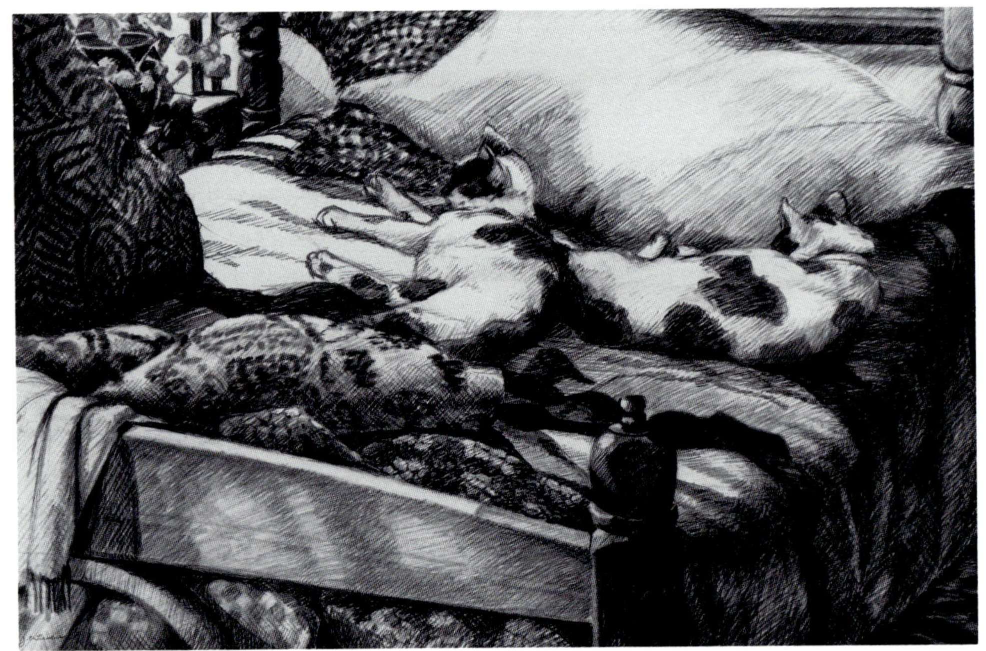

"DOUBLE PORTRAIT OF SASHA" 1980

CHARCOAL
29" × 40"

A N N E   C .   W E B E R

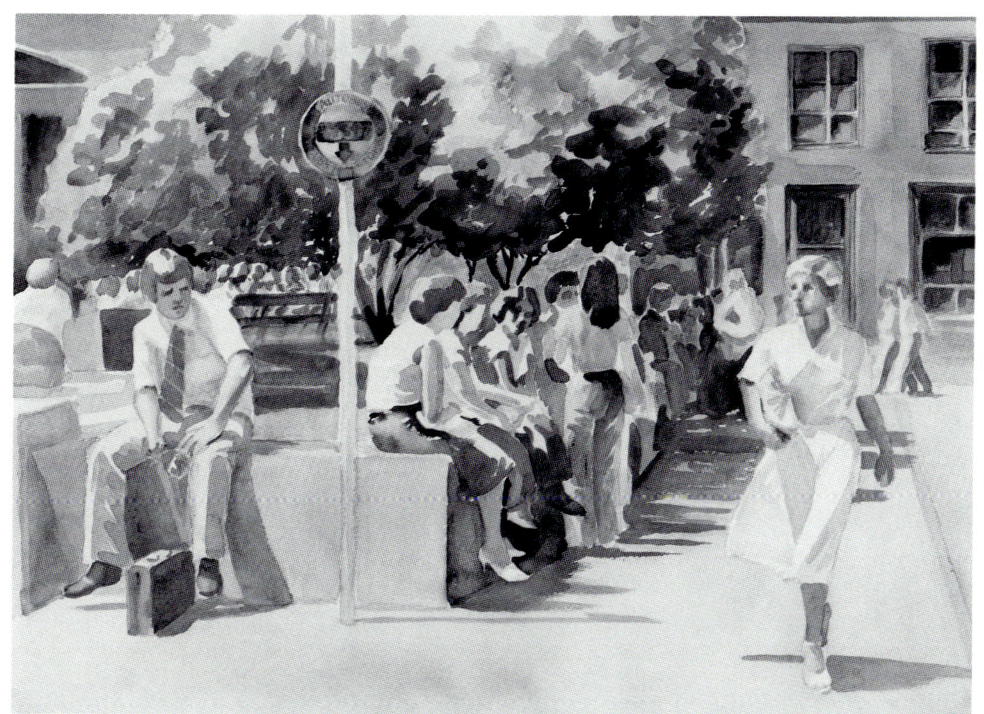

"M O N T R E A L   B U S   S T O P"   1 9 8 0

WATERCOLOR
29″ × 36″

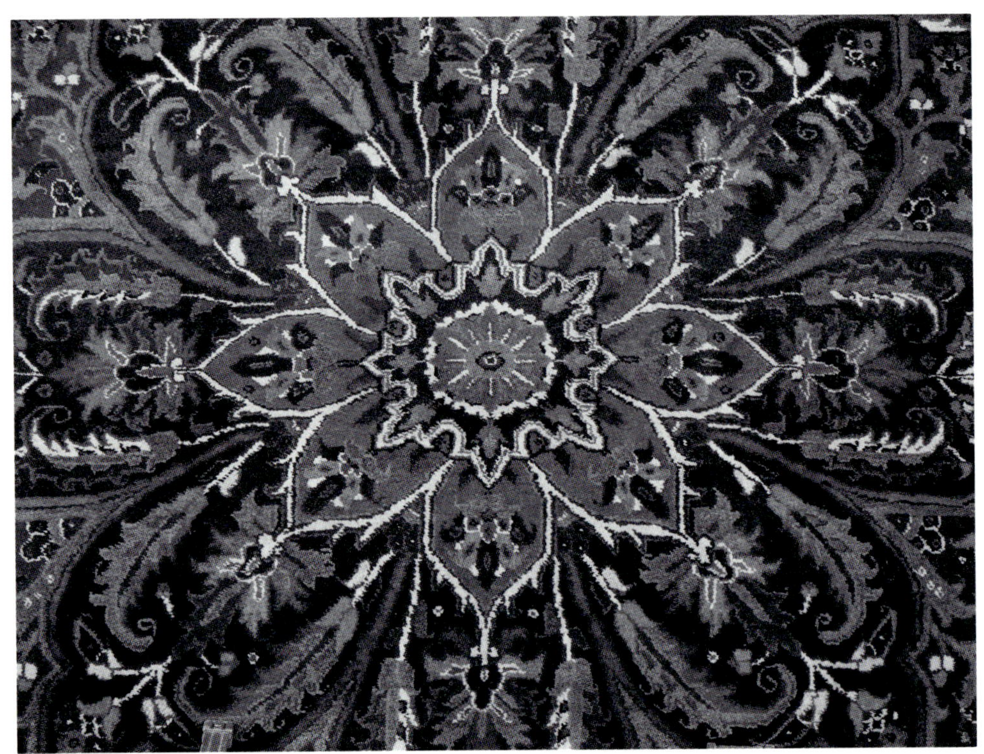

"AHAR HERIZ ORIENTAL RUG" CIRCA 1934

HANDWOVEN, WOOL
10′ × 14′

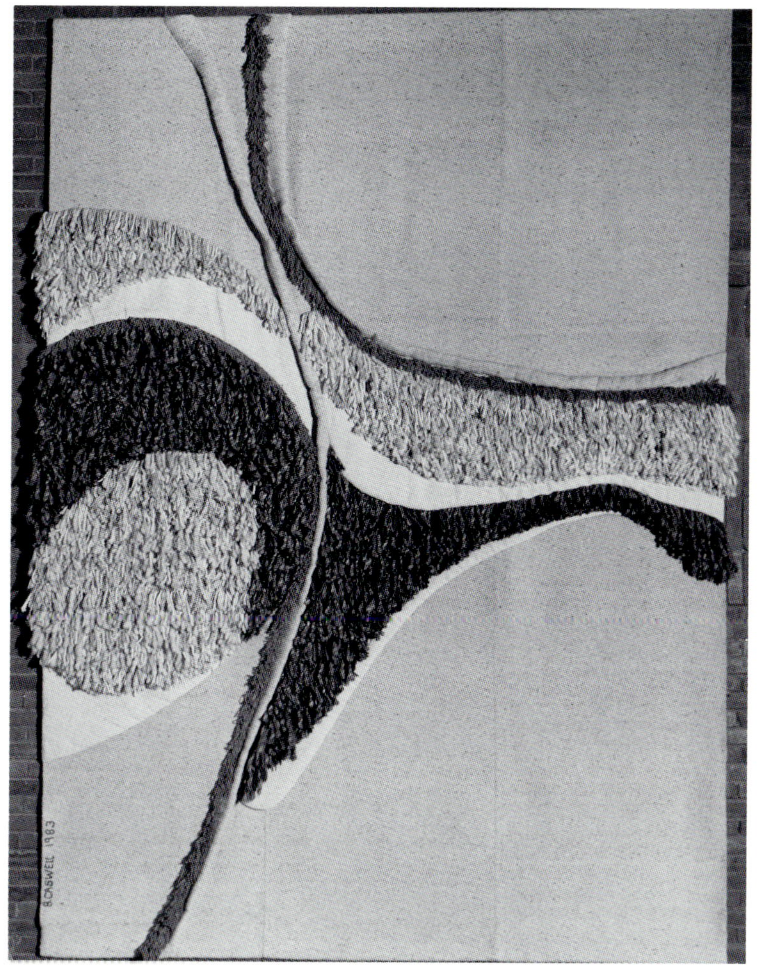

"U N T I T L E D   W A L L H A N G I N G"   1 9 8 3

HANDWOVEN, WOOL AND LINEN
12′ × 9′ × 6″

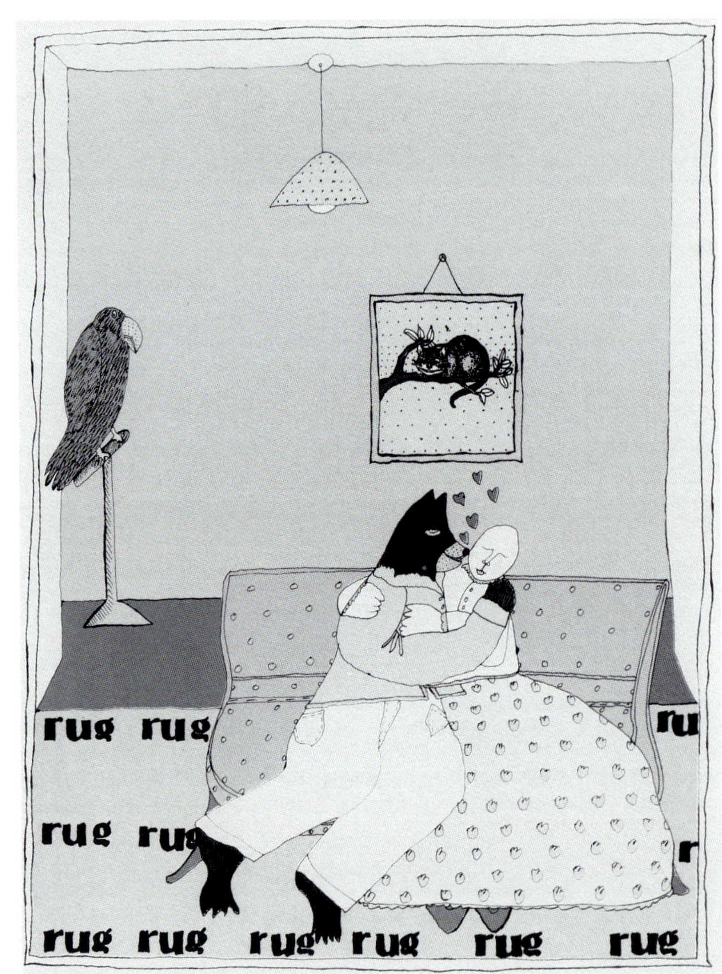

"R U G ,   R U G ,   R U G "   1 9 8 2

SILKSCREEN
22″ × 15″

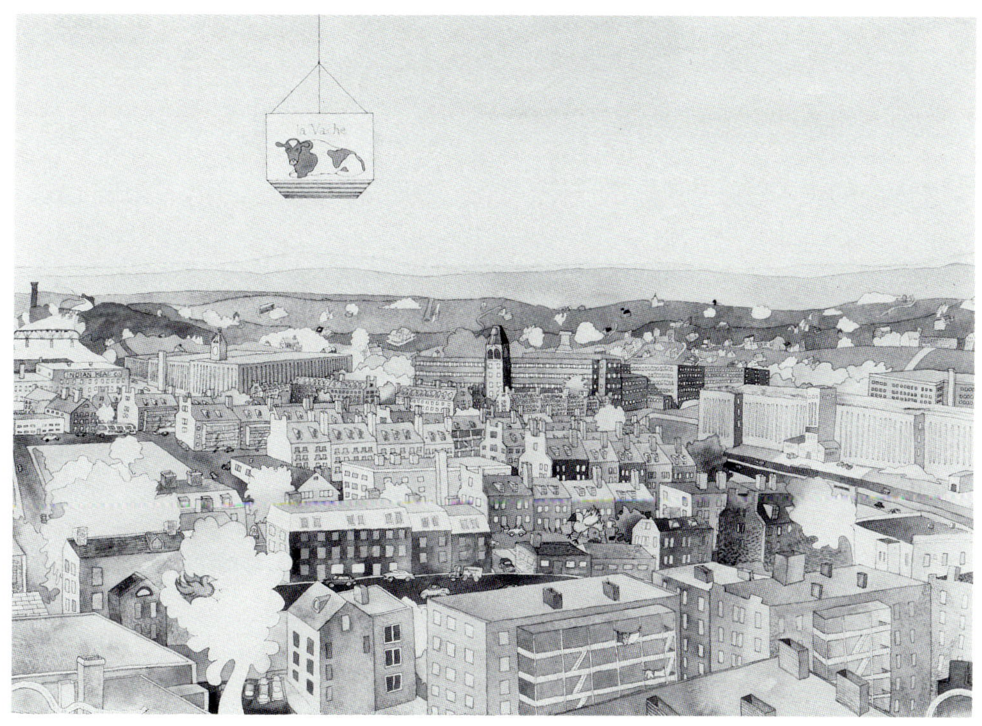

"MANCHESTER ET LA VACHE" 1979-80

WATERCOLOR
25" × 34"

LEE A. SCHUETTE
AND ASSOCIATE RICK MCAULAY

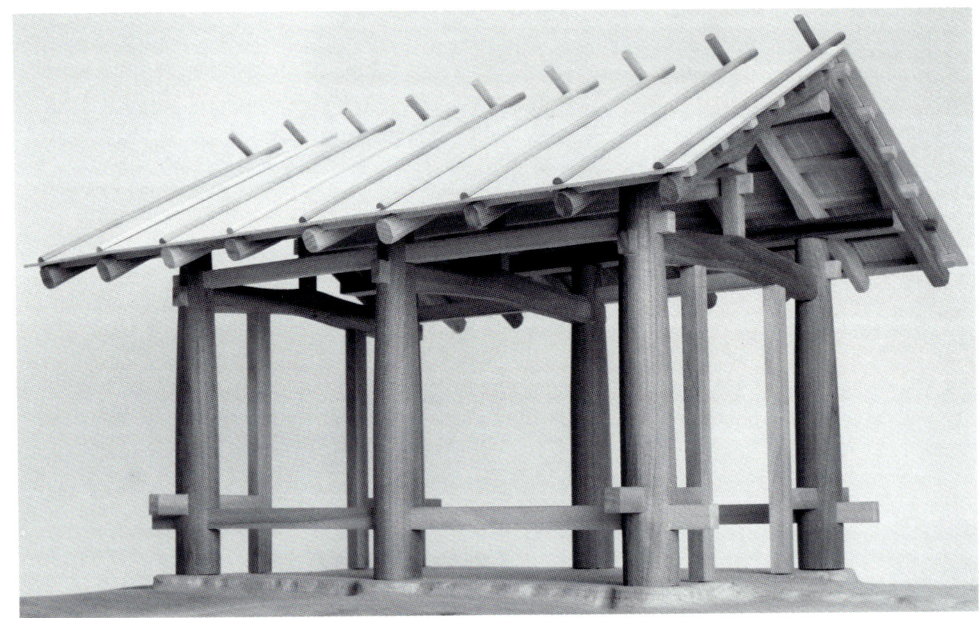

MODEL FOR "TEAHOUSE PAVILLION" 1988

NATIVE PINE, WHITE OAK, COPPER
12′ × 7′ × 15′

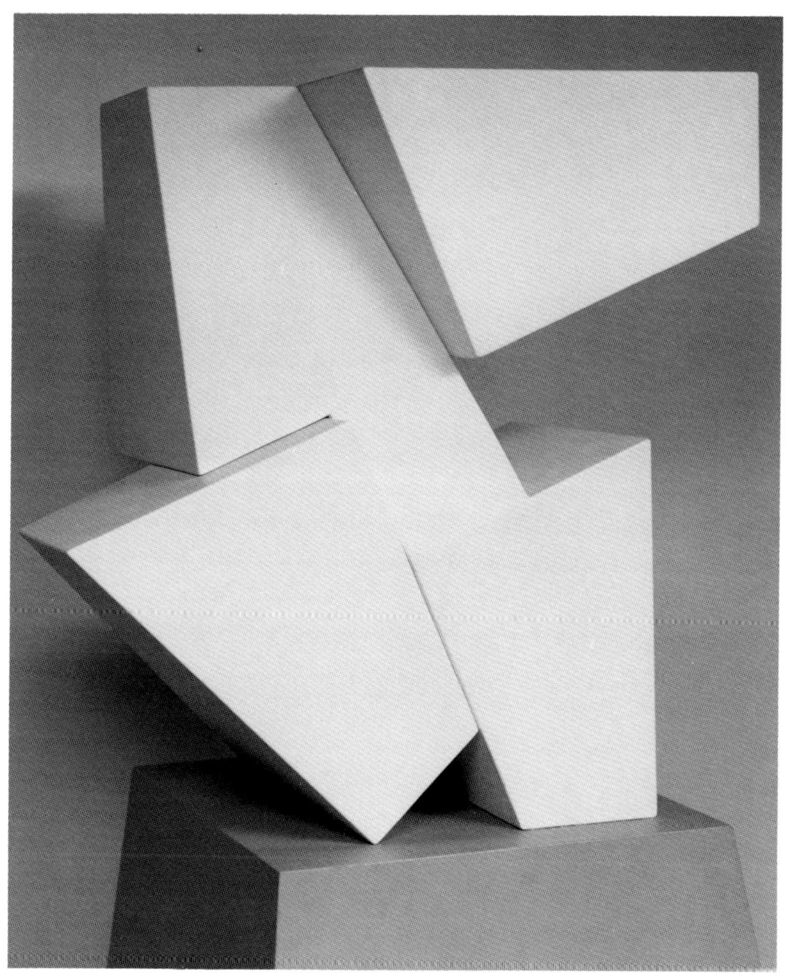

"C O N C O R D   # 4 4 "   1 9 8 3

CORETEN STEEL
40″ × 42″ × 24″

DAVID FULLAM

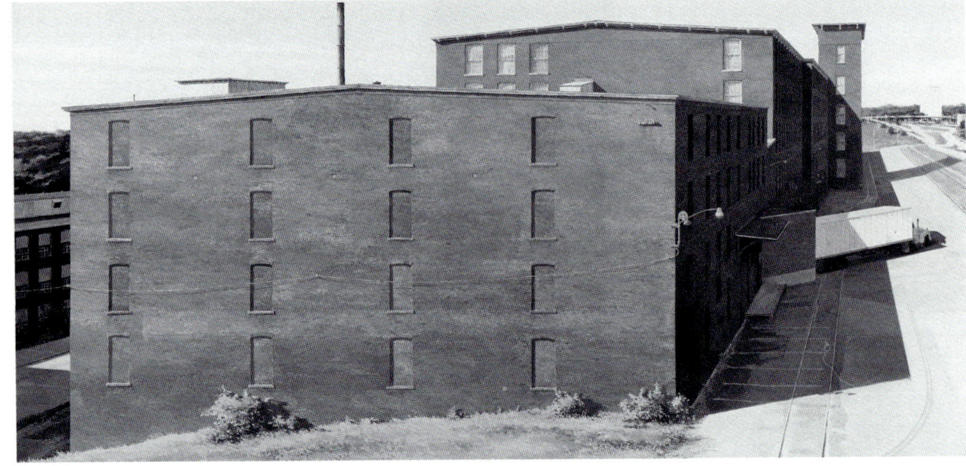

"MILLYARD" 1982

GOUACHE PAINTING
28¼" × 46¼"

J U D I T H   W I L B O U R   N E L S O N

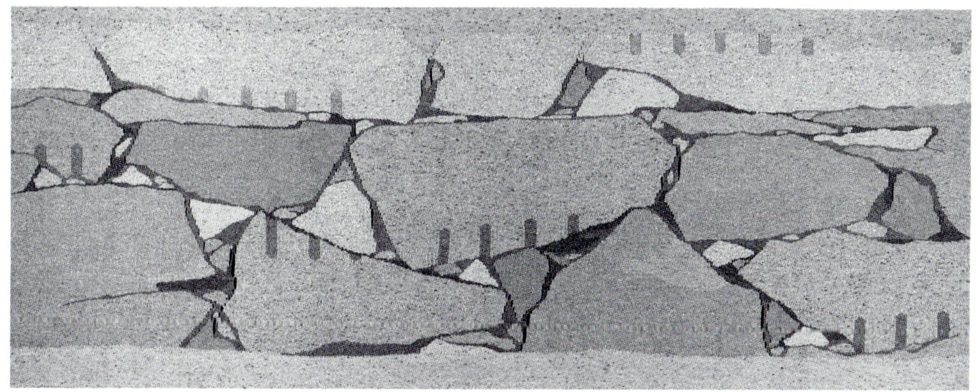

"S T O N E W A L L   T A P E S T R Y"   1 9 8 4

HANDWOVEN, WOOL AND COTTON
42″ × 9′

B O B   L A P R E E

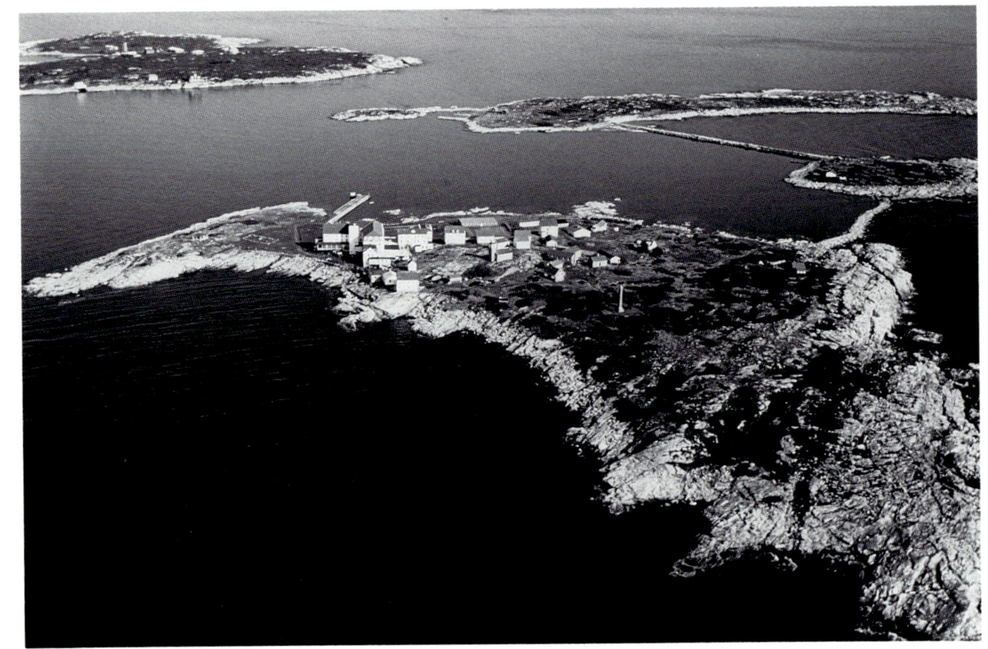

"I S L E S   O F   S H O A L S"   1 9 7 7

CIBACHROME PHOTOGRAPH
11″ × 14″

E S T H E R   A M E L I A   T I T C O M B

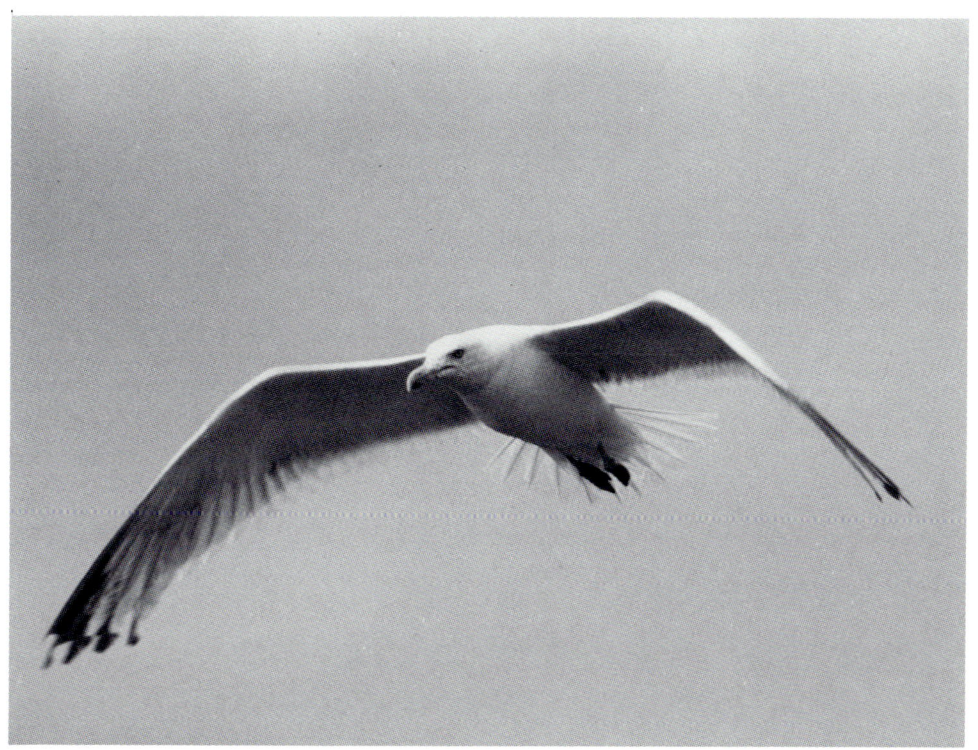

"J O U R N E Y   E A S T W A R D"   1 9 8 4

BLACK AND WHITE PHOTOGRAPH
11″ × 14″

CONLEY HARRIS

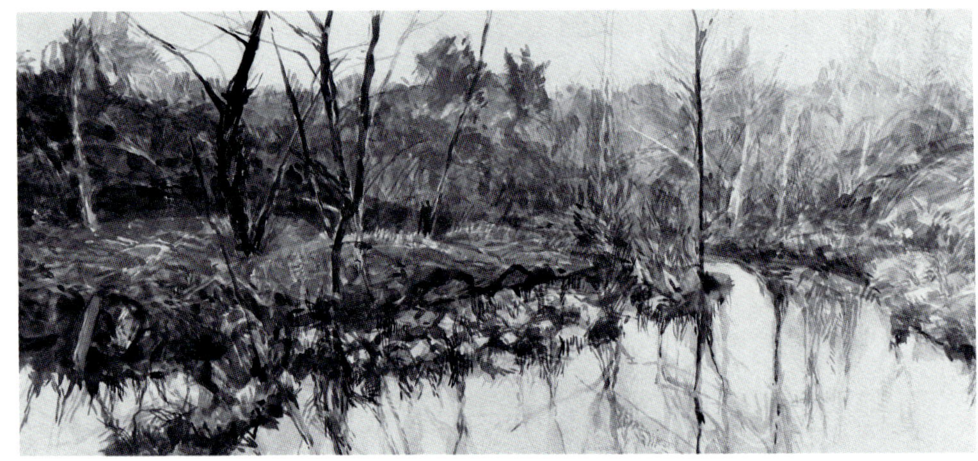

"SHIMMERING MARSH" 1984

WATERCOLOR
25″ × 82″

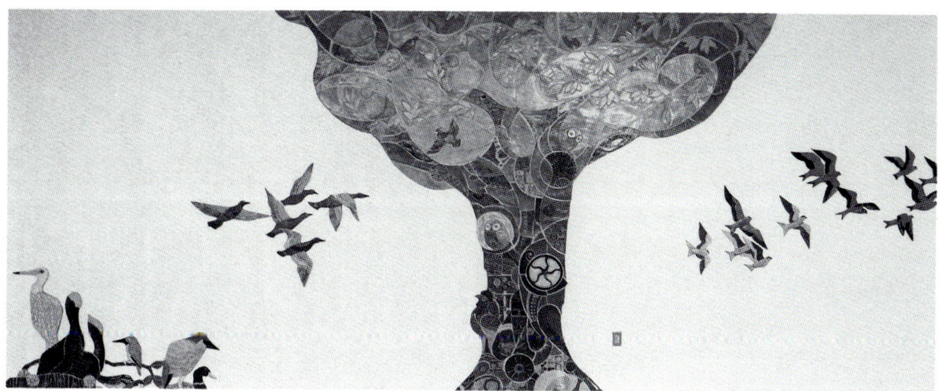

"T R E E   A N D   B I R D S"   M U R A L   1 9 8 6

HANDMADE CLAY TILES
10'8" × 25'4"

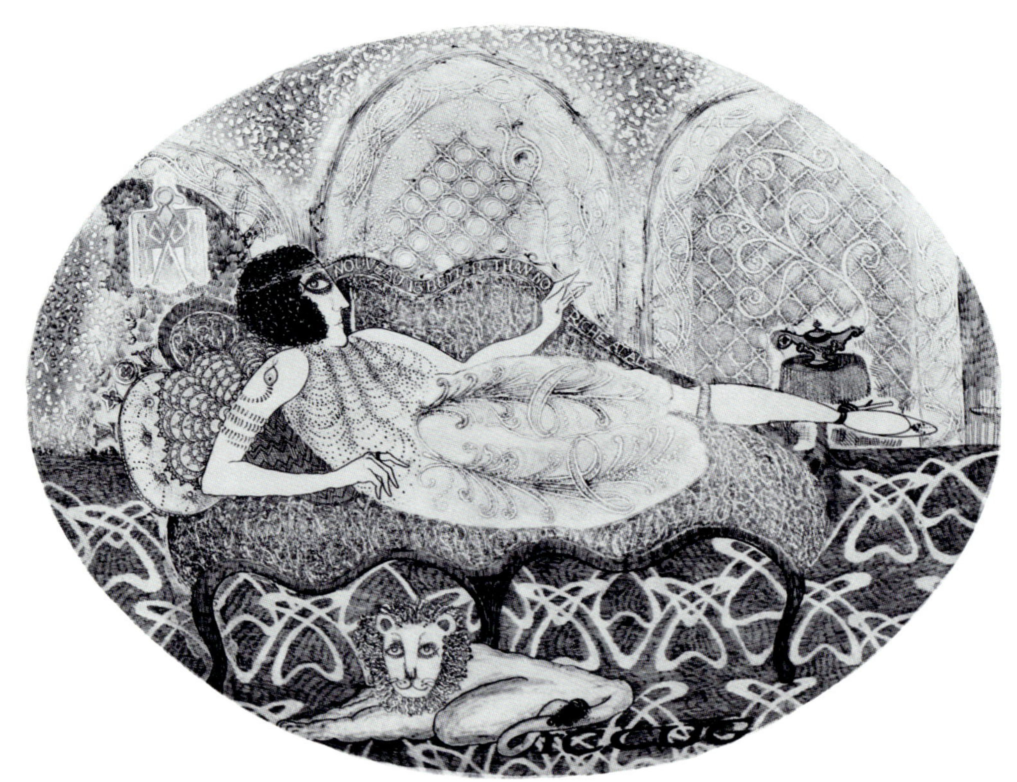

"BETWEEN INHERITANCES" 1981

INTAGLIO PRINT
20″ × 24″

DIMITRI GERAKARIS

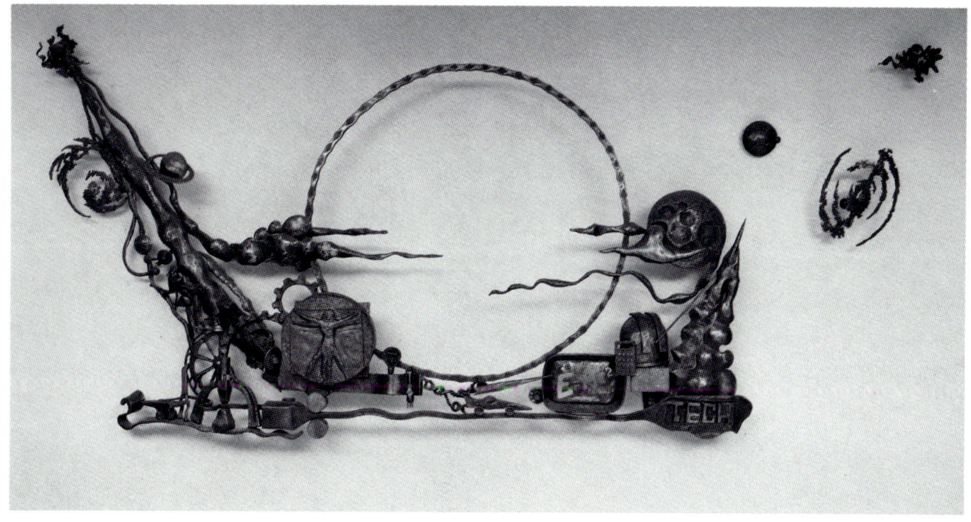

"TECHNOVERSE" 1983

FORGED STEEL
4′ × 9′

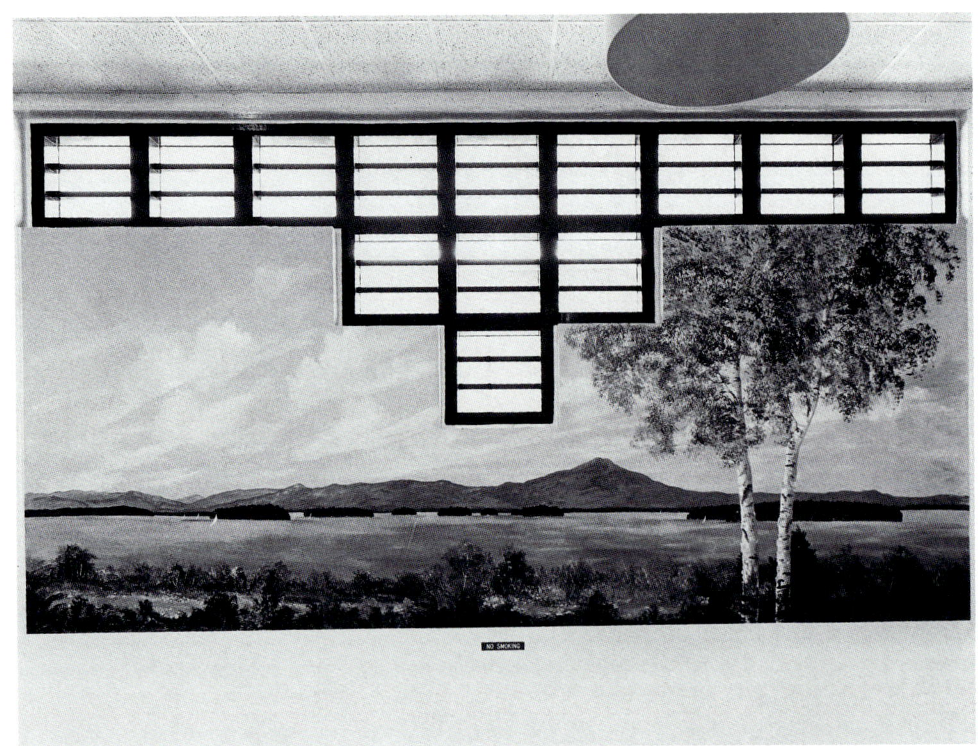

" S C E N I C   L A K E   W I N N I P E S A U K E E   S U M M E R   V I E W "   1 9 8 5

ACRYLIC ON CEMENT BLOCK
6′ × 15′

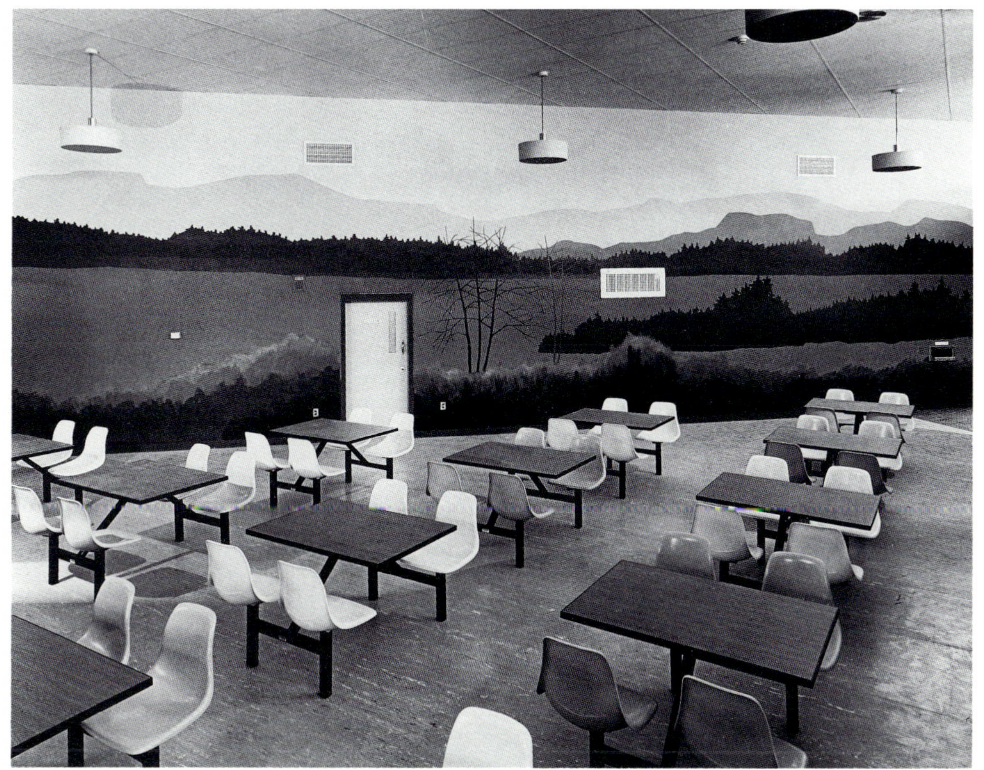

"LANDSCAPE" 1985

ACRYLIC ON CEMENT BLOCK
16′ × 48′

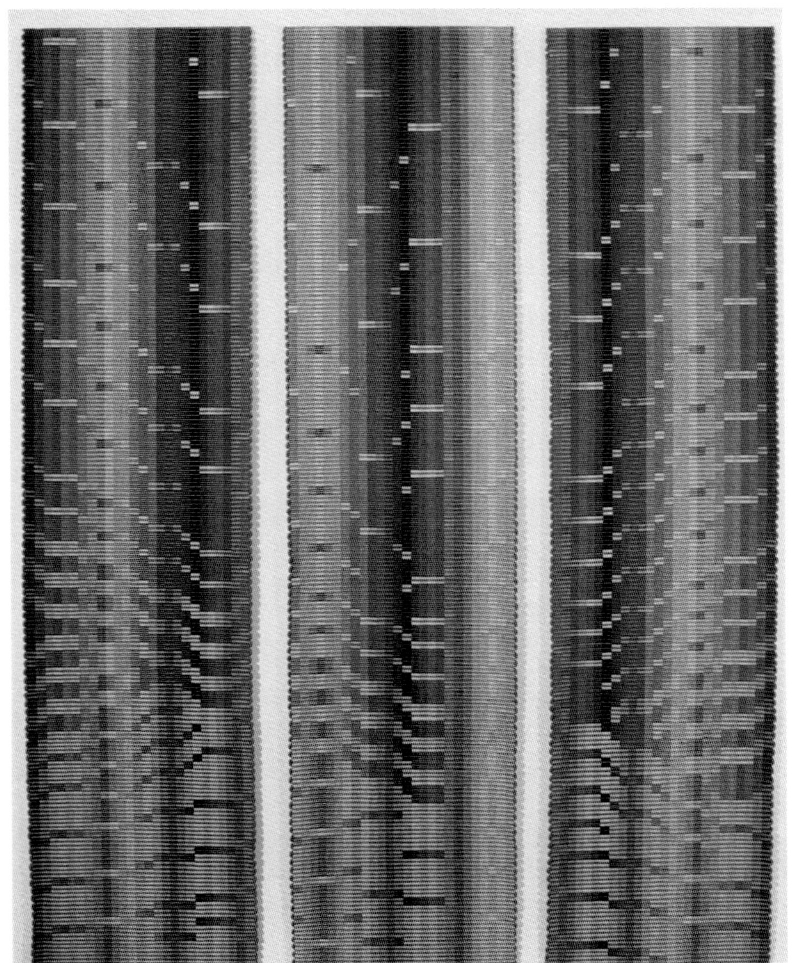

"C H O I C E S"   1 9 8 6

HANDWOVEN COTTON
6½' × 4½'

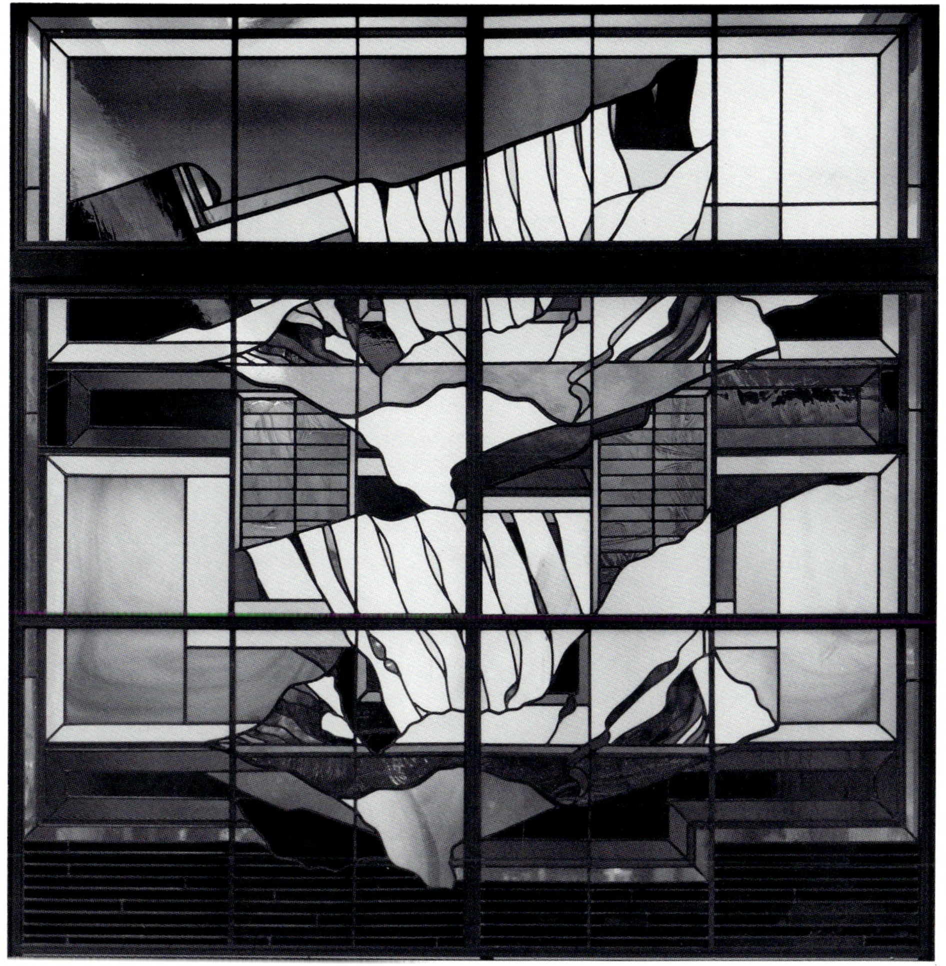

"S E A C O A S T   E V O L U T I O N"   1 9 8 4

MOUTHBLOWN ANTIQUE GLASS
82″ × 78″

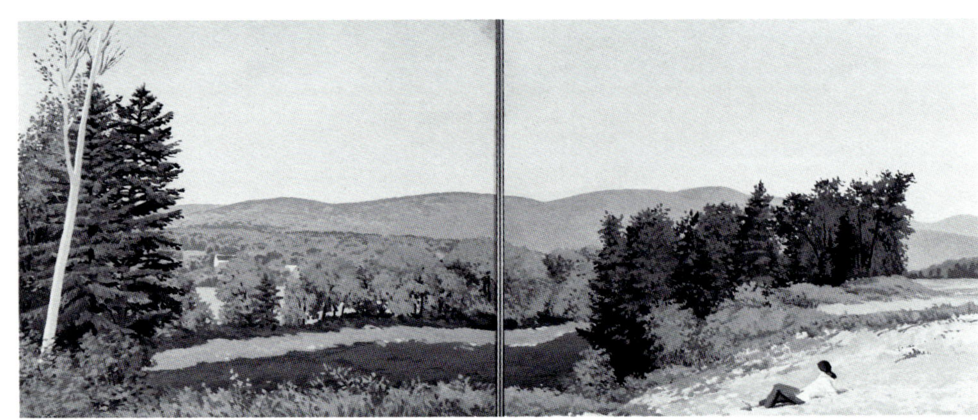

"VERMONT LANDSCAPE WITH FIGURE" 1972

OIL ON CANVAS
30" × 60"

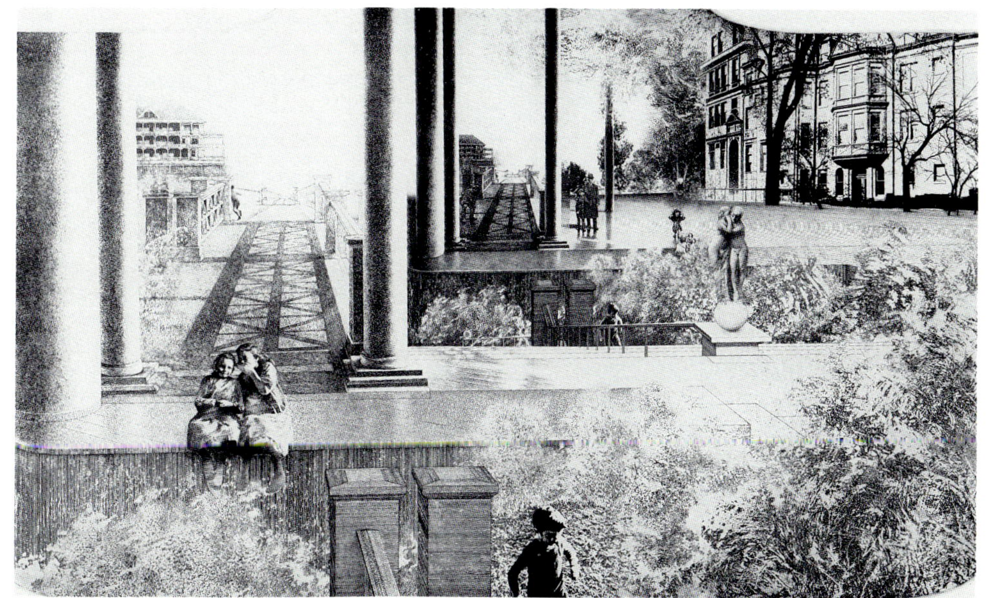

"FIRST GATE" 1974

ETCHING
20″ × 30″

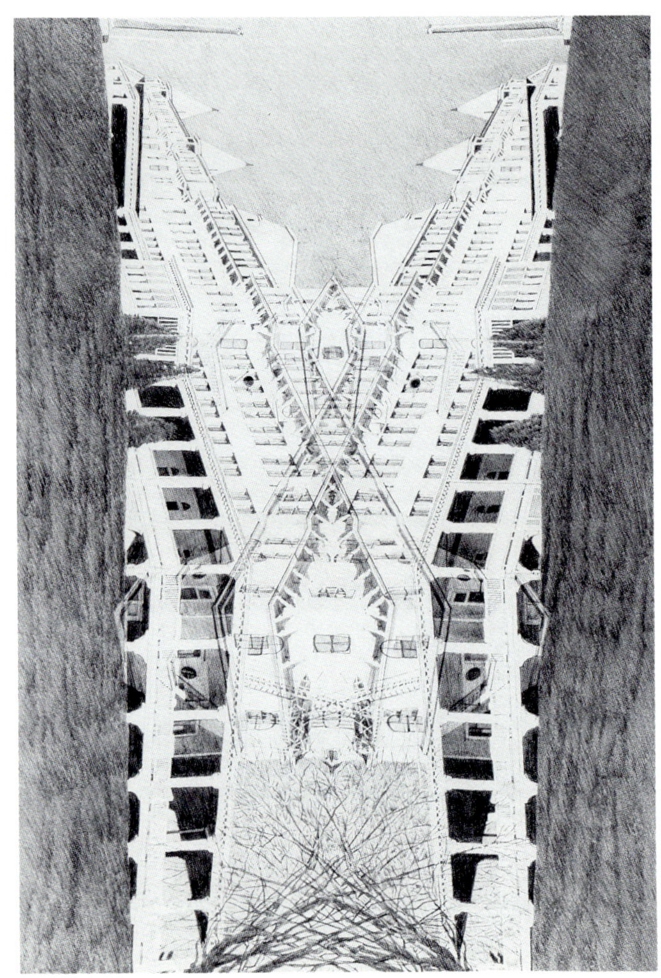

" W E N T W O R T H   W O N D E R   # 2 "   1 9 8 0

PENCIL
24″ × 16″

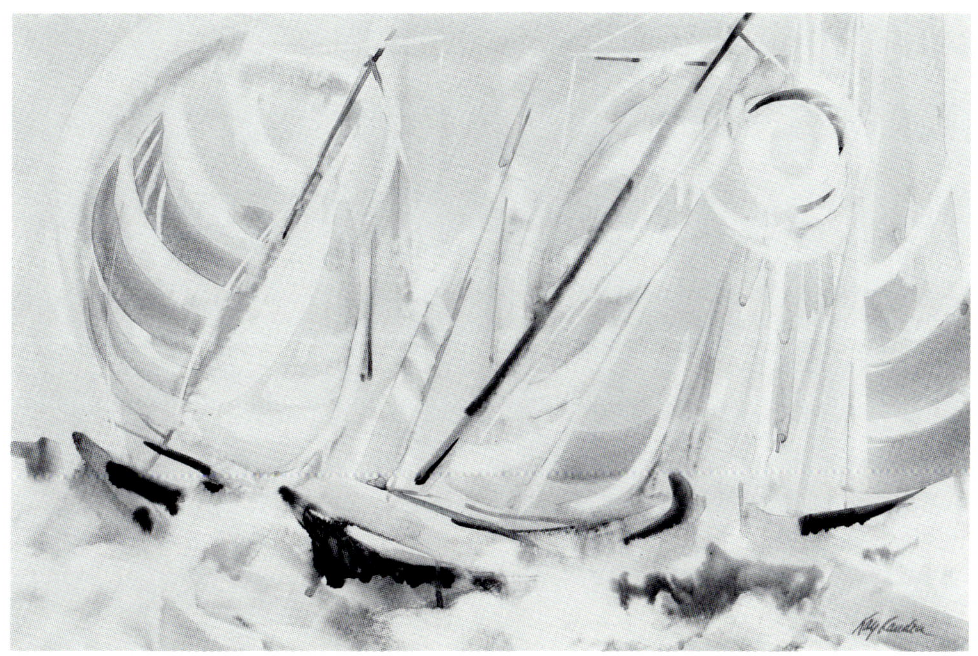

"S A I L B O A T   R A C E   # 3"

WATERCOLOR
20″ × 30″

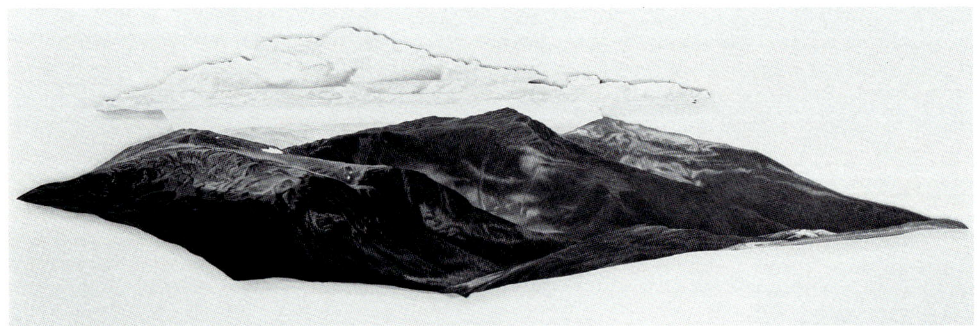

" J E F F E R S O N ,   A D A M S ,   A N D   M A D I S O N   F R O M   T H E
M T .   W A S H I N G T O N   A U T O   R O A D ,   L A T E   A F T E R N O O N ,
4   J U L Y   " 8 2 "   1 9 8 3

OIL ON SHAPED COTTON CANVAS
4'11" × 17' × 1½"

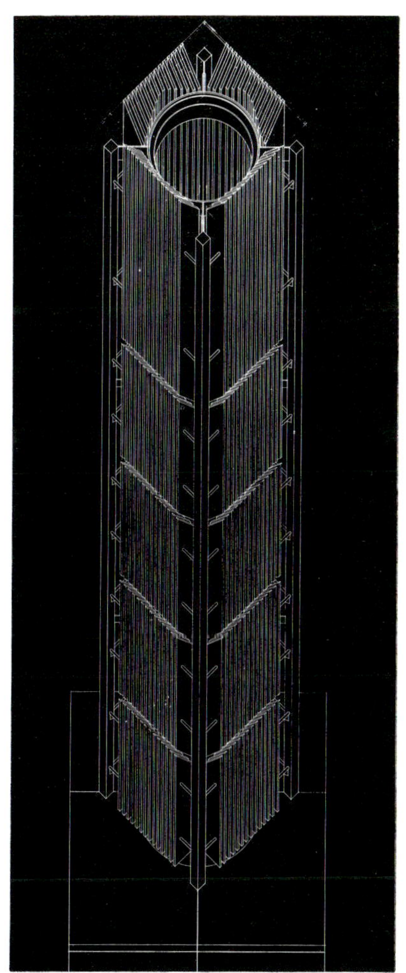

S T U D Y   F O R   " G L A S S   F O U N T A I N   A N D   B E N C H "   1 9 8 9

GLASS, DICHROIC GLASS ACCENT
17′ × 3′ × 3′
GRANITE BENCH
18″ × 5′ × 5′

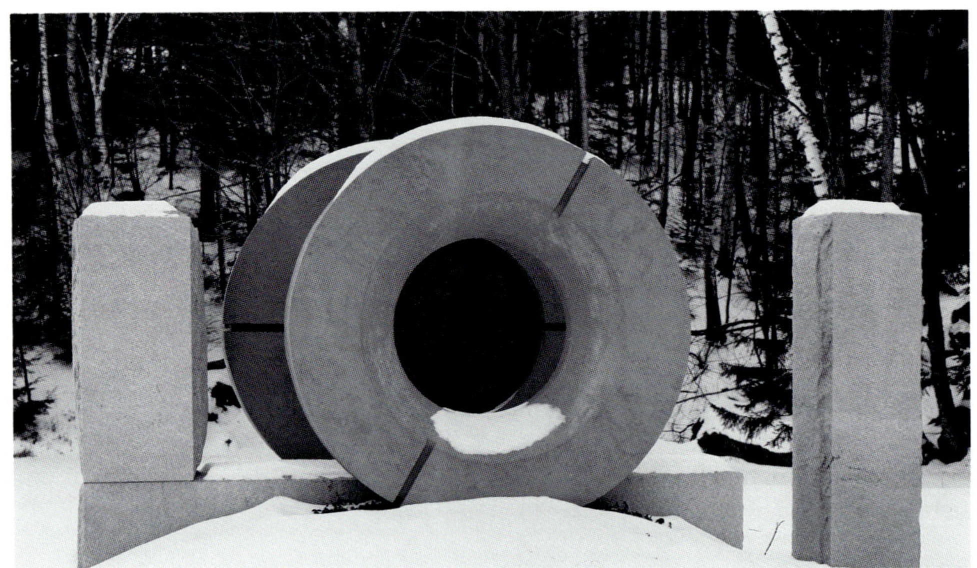

"SUNAPEE MANDALA" 1986

CAST CONCRETE, CLAY AND GRANITE
10′ × 17′ × 13′

MARIE HARRIS

LEAVE YOUR SHADOW HERE

ON THE LONG MEMORY OF ROCK

THAT YOU MAY NUMBER AMONG

THE FRIENDS OF THIS PLANET:

WE ARE ONE

IN SUMMER WOODS

OVERFLOWING WITH WINGS,

IN THE FIRES KINDLED

BY ORANGE LILY STRUCK

AGAINST FERN FLINT,

ONE WITH THE MUSIC OF WIND

PLAYED ON ICY BIRCH BONES,

AND THE PROMISE POLLEN SPELLS

ACROSS THE WATERY MIRRORS

OF OUR FUTURE.

POEM FOR "SUNAPEE MANDALA" 1986

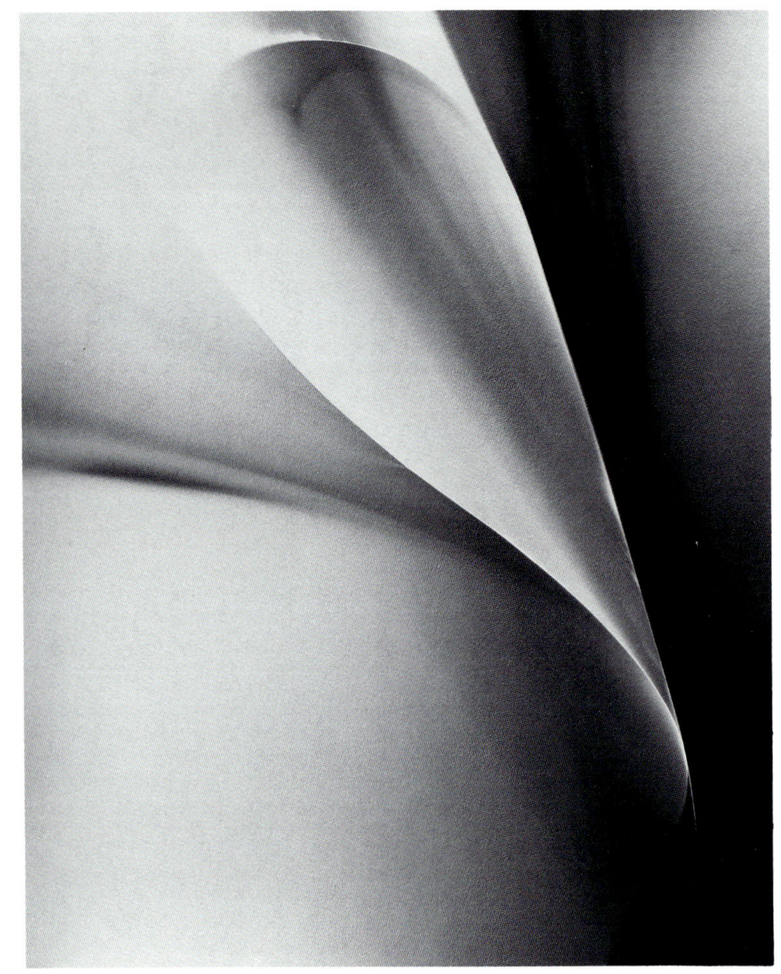

"U N T I T L E D"   C I R C A   1 9 4 5 - 1 9 6 5

CAMERA-LESS PHOTOGENIC
10″ × 8″

The Arts Bank Collection grew in response to a need to spread limited state art funds to the greatest number of sites possible. The solution was to develop a collection of portable art works that could travel around the state. Thanks to a percentage of funds generated from new construction at the New Hampshire State Prison in 1984, more than 180 works of art were purchased and organized into an exhibition. The exhibition toured for three years, appearing at 22 sites from Dover to Claremont and from Berlin to Nashua. In 1989 the Arts Bank Collection was taken off tour to be distributed to permanent locations around the state.

Arts Bank Artists

Sigmund Abeles
John P. Adams
Shawn Allen
Martha Andrea
Jane Banquer
Loretta S.W. Barnett
Thomas R. Barrett
Katy Baucke
Tom Blackwell
John Bott
Boulanger and Freres*
Ulric Bourgeois*
Eleanor Briggs
Kay Brown
James H. Burgess
R. Alden Burt
Adrienne Campbell
Gordon B. Carlisle
David M. Carroll
Robert M. Chace
Pat Lowery Collins
Jean-Denis Cruchet
Becky Darling
Ellen M. Davison
Nancy DeYoung
Sandra Dold
Blanche Dombek
John Terrence Downs
Anne Dubois
Jayne Dwyer
James M. Fortune
A.H.R. Foss*
Norman Francoeur
Thomas P. Glover
Melinda Greason
A. Gregory*
Elizabeth S. Gurrier
Peter Hall
Conley Harris
John W. Hatch
William Haust
Susanne F. Holcombe
Rick Hunt
Robi Glaser Jackson
Lotte Jacobi
Peder Johnson

Richard C. Johnson
William H. Johnson
Robert Jordan
Carol Jowdy
Kay Kandra
Geoffrey Katz
Johanna Kent
Christopher Kressy
Adrienne LaVallee
Donald Lent
Judith Lerner
Steven W. Lewis
Calvin J. Libby
David F. MacEachran
John MacIver
Robert T. Malinowski
Fran Mallon
Leni Mancuso
Peter Maurer
Allan P. McCulloch
Chase McNiss
Thomas H. Meyers
Randy Miller
Annette Mitchell
Pat Moran
Frank Moulton
Nancy Nemec
David Niles, Jr.
Erik R. Nilsen

Lorraine Koch Palmer
W. H. Parish*
Nadine Perry
David A. Plante
Paul Pollaro
Peter E. Randall
David Richman
Scott Riel
John E. Roberts
William C. Roy
Eric M. Sanford
Scott Schnepf
Kit Semmes
Ann Semprebon
Julie S. Serrano
Eric F. Sinclair
Richard T. Slater
Gail Smuda
Mary Margaret Sweeney
Mary C. Taylor
Chuck Theodore
Janis E. Theodore
Ann Thompson
Esther Amelia Titcomb
Harry Umen
Marguerite Walsh Umen
Mavis Viles
Herbert O. Waters
Anne C. Weber
Fleur Weymouth
Stuart H. Williams
Ricker Windsor
Thomas C. Woodbury
Arthur Yanoff
Nancy Zieske

Active in the late 19th and early 20th centuries

Locations of illustrated artworks are noted at the bottom of each biography.

NHAA refers to New Hampshire Art Association's annual exhibition at The Currier Gallery of Art.

John P. Adams   24, 45

Newington, NH

Place of birth:
Laconia, NH
July 5, 1932

Undergraduate:
Franklin Institute of Professional Photography, Boston, MA, 1957

Art awards:
Dorothy Eames Award, NH
Professional Photographers
Association
Industrial Photographers of America
Award, 1978, 1979, 1980, 1985, 1987
University Photographers
Association of America
(22 awards) 1968-1985

Permanent collections:
Arts Bank
State of New Hampshire

Corporate collections:
Laconia Savings Bank
Laconia, NH

Dover Federal Savings Bank
Durham, NH

Wentworth Douglas Hospital
Dover, NH

Major exhibitions/publications:
Author, *Bottle Collecting in New England,* 1969
Author, *Bottle Collecting in America,* 1972
John P. Adams' *Third Bottle Book,* 1972
Drowned Valley: The Piscataqua River Basin, 1976
25th Anniversary of the University System of New Hampshire: Visions for Tomorrow, 1988

Current educational affiliation:
University Photographer, 1969-1988

Public/site-specific art work locations:
NH Vocational-Technical College
Stratham, NH

Carol Aronson   16

Portsmouth, NH

Place of birth:
Chicago, IL
May 27, 1941

Undergraduate:
Boston University, BFA, 1963

Graduate:
University of Chicago, MA, 1965

Art awards:
Bellinger Memorial Award,
Chautauqua National, 1984
Costello Memorial Award, NHAA,
1983
Award of Merit, Biennial National
Meadows Museum of Art, 1982

Permanent collections:
Roberson Center for the Arts
& Sciences
Binghamton, NY

Corporate collections:
F French Investing Company
New York, NY

Major exhibitions:
One Woman Show
Pindar Gallery
New York, NY

27th National Exhibition of
American Art
Chautauqua Art Association
Chautauqua, NY

Regional Selections 83
Hood Museum
Hanover, NH

Gallery affiliations:
Pindar Gallery
New York, NY

Current educational affiliation:
University of New Hampshire
Durham, NH
Associate Professor

Public/site-specific art work locations:
NH Fish & Game Department
Concord, NH

Henry Marcel Bakula   43

Kittery, ME

Place of birth:
Boston, MA
January 16, 1916

Undergraduate:
Scott Carbee School of Art,
Boston, MA

Art awards:
Best of Show, York Art Association,
1981
Grumbacher Award, York Art
Association
Best of Show, Littleton, NH

Permanent collections:
Daniel J. Pitot
Kittery, ME

David Mann
Kittery, ME

Governor John H. Sununu
Salem, NH

Corporate collections:
BankEast
Portsmouth, NH

Indian Head Bank
Portsmouth, NH

Hampton Cooperative Bank
Hampton, NH

Gallery affiliations:
Bakula Studios & Gallery
Kittery, ME

Public/site-specific art work locations:
NH Vocational-Technical College
Stratham, NH

Emile Birch   78

Canaan, NH

Place of birth:
Providence, RI
July 28, 1947

Undergraduate:
The Brooklyn Museum Art School,
Brooklyn, NY, 1973-74
Arts Students League, New York,
NY, 1969-71
Rhode Island School of Design,
Providence, RI, 1967-68

Art awards:
Scholarship, Rhode Island School
of Design
Scholarship, Museum of Fine Arts,
Boston
Representative for the State of New
Hampshire, National Very Special
Arts Festival, Washington, DC, 1984

Corporate collections:
Chubb LifeAmerica
Concord, NH

CREARE, Inc.
Hanover, NH

Current educational affiliation:
Artist-in-Residence Program
NH State Council on the Arts

Public/site-specific art work locations:
Franconia Notch State Park
Franconia, NH

Town of Exeter
Exeter, NH

Mount Sunapee State Park
NH Division of Parks & Recreation
Sunapee, NH

Place of birth:
New York, NY
November 16, 1939

Undergraduate:
Sweetbriar College, Sweetbriar,
VA, 1961

Art awards:
Signal Companies Award, NHAA,
1983
Merit Award, LaGrange National,
LaGrange College, Louisiana, 1984
NH Chapter American Institute of
Architects, NHAA, 1987

Permanent collections:
Arts Bank
State of New Hampshire

Smith College Museum of Art
Northampton, MA

The Currier Gallery of Art
Manchester, NH

Corporate collections:
Peterborough Savings Bank
Peterborough, NH

Major exhibitions:
New England Now, 1987
DeCordova and Dana Museum
Lincoln, MA

In Spite of Everything, Yes, 1986
Hood Museum of Art
Hanover, NH

The Currier Gallery of Art, 1984
Manchester, NH

Gallery affiliation:
AVA Gallery
Hanover, NH

**Public/site-specific art work
locations:**
NH Vocational-Technical College
Manchester, NH

Place of birth:
Concord, NH
March 31, 1953

Undergraduate:
University of New Hampshire,
Durham, NH, BA 1975

Art awards:
Art Festival Award, Westport,
CT, 1978

Major exhibitions:
The Manchester Institute of Arts
and Sciences
2nd, 4th & 5th New Hampshire
Arts Biennial
Manchester, NH

Artworks Gallery
Boston, MA

Richard Mitton Memorial
Exhibition, 1974
Boston, MA

Current educational affiliation:
Notre Dame College
Manchester, NH
Instructor, Illustration

**Public/site-specific art work
locations:**
Health & Human Services Building
Concord, NH

Place of birth:
Boothbay Harbor, ME
July 21, 1943

Undergraduate:
University of New Hampshire,
Durham, NH, BA 1965

Graduate:
Indiana University, Bloomington,
IN, MFA 1967

Permanent collections:
Addison Gallery of American Art
Andover, MA

Art In Embassy Program
Washington, DC

Pacific Securities International
Los Angeles, CA

Corporate collections:
Chase Manhattan Bank
New York, NY

Prudential Insurance Company
Newark, NJ

General Electric
Fairfield, CT

Major exhibitions:
Retrospective Exhibition, 1966-1986
Addison Gallery of American Art
Andover, MA

Holly Solomon Gallery, 1976, 1978,
1980, 1984
New York, NY

Fujii Gallery, 1984, 1988
Tokyo, Japan

Gallery affiliation:
Howard Yezerski Gallery
Boston, MA

Current educational affiliation:
School of Visual Arts
New York, NY
Instructor, Graduate Workshop

**Public/site-specific art work
locations:**
NH Vocational-Technical College
Laconia, NH

Place of birth:
New York, NY
November 20, 1929

Undergraduate:
Cooper Union, New York, NY
Studied with Alexi Brodovitch,
Berenice Abbott, Joseph Breitersbach,
and Harold Feinstein

Art awards:
Purchase Prize, Howe Library, 1982

Permanent collections:
Arts Bank
State of New Hampshire

Major exhibitions/publications:
One Person Show
Colby-Sawyer College
New London, NH

Deming Art Gallery
New London, NH

Photographer for *Using the Potter's
Wheel*, Van Nostrand Reinhold

**Educational affiliation/work
experience:**
Design and photo research for
Harcourt, Brace & Jovanovich,
McGraw Hill, and Ginn and
Company, 1954-1960

**Public/site-specific art work
locations:**
NH Vocational-Technical College
Stratham, NH

Gordon B. Carlisle　　51

Portsmouth, NH

Place of birth:
Passaic, NJ
March 11, 1951

Undergraduate:
San Francisco Art Institute,
San Francisco, CA, BFA 1973

Art awards:
First Place, Prescott Park Art Festival,
Portsmouth, NH, 1988

Permanent collections:
The Currier Gallery of Art
Manchester, NH

Concord Hospital
Concord, NH

Arts Bank
State of New Hampshire

Corporate collections:
Chubb LifeAmerica
Concord, NH

Major exhibitions:
The Studio Exhibition,
1986, 1987, 1988
Portsmouth, NH

Gallery affiliation:
Blackthorn Gallery
Portsmouth, NH

**Public/site-specific art work
locations:**
New Hampshire Building/NH
Department of Agriculture
Eastern States Fairgrounds
West Springfield, MA

United Savings Bank
Manchester, NH

NH Savings Bank
Concord, NH

Concord Hospital
Concord, NH

James Fraser Carpenter　　77

North Haven, ME

Place of birth:
Washington, DC
April 11, 1949

Undergraduate:
Choate School, Wallingford, CT,
1968, School Art Prize
Rhode Island School of Design,
BFA 1972, European Honors Program

Art awards:
Fellowship, National Endowment for
the Arts, 1976, 1988

Permanent collections:
Metropolitan Museum of Art
New York, NY

Corning Museum of Glass
Corning, NY

San Francisco Museum of Art
San Francisco, CA

Corporate collections:
Coca-Cola Company
Atlanta, GA

Hoffman-LaRouche
Geneva, Switzerland

JMB
Chicago, IL

Major exhibitions:
Architectural Art, 1988
New York, NY

Current educational affiliation:
Royal College of Art
London, England
Associate Lecturer

**Public/site-specific art work
locations:**
Portland Center for Performing Arts
Portland, OR

CTS
Indianapolis, IN

3600 Market Street
Philadelphia, PA

New Hampshire Hospital
Concord, NH

Brenda Caswell　　55

Meredith, NH

Place of birth:
Claremont, NH
January 1, 1954

Undergraduate:
Plymouth State College, Plymouth,
NH, BFA 1976

Major exhibitions:
1st Annual Regional Selections
Jaffe Fried Gallery
Hopkins Center
Hanover, NH

One Woman Show
Lamson Gallery
Plymouth, NH

Marian Graves-Mugar Art Gallery
Colby-Sawyer College
New London, NH

Gallery affiliation:
Horizons Art Gallery
Campton, NH

**Public/site-specific art work
locations:**
Health and Human Services Building
Concord, NH

Loon Mountain Club
Lincoln, NH

Bruno Civitico　　72

Charlestown, SC

Place of birth:
Dignano, D'Istria, Italy
September 1, 1942

Undergraduate:
Pratt Institute, BFA 1966

Graduate:
Indiana University, MFA, 1968

Art awards:
Guggenheim Fellowship, 1979
Fellowship, National Endowment for
the Arts, 1980
Louis Comfort Tiffany Prize in
Painting, 1981

Permanent collections:
Bayly Museum
Charlottesville, VA

Boston Public Library
Boston, MA

Claude Bernard Galleries
New York, NY

Corporate collections:
Chubb LifeAmerica
Concord, NH

Bank of New Hampshire
Manchester, NH

Chemical Bank of New York
New York, NY

Major exhibitions:
5 One Man Shows
R. Schoelkopf Gallery
New York, NY

New American Realists
Rome, Italy

American Figure Drawing
Adelide & Melbourne, Australia

Gallery affiliation:
Contemporary Realist Gallery
San Francisco, CA

**Public/site-specific art work
locations:**
Health and Human Services Building
Concord, NH

Jean-Denis Cruchet   17

Harrisville, NH

Place of birth:
Lausanne, Switzerland
November 9, 1939

Undergraduate:
Beaux-Arts, Geneva, Switzerland,
Degree in sculpture

Graduate:
Scola Brera, studied with Marino
Marini, Milan, Italy

Permanent collections:
The Currier Gallery of Art
Manchester, NH

Smith College Museum of Art
Northampton, MA

Beaux-Arts Museum
Lausanne, Switzerland

Arts Bank
State of New Hampshire

Corporate collections:
Alexandrite Corporation at the
Commerce Center
Houston, TX

Major exhibitions:
Three Man Show
Galerie Numaga
Auvernier, Switzerland

30 One Man Shows in Europe and
the United States
1962 to present

Gallery affiliation:
Franz Bader
Washington, DC

**Public/site-specific art work
locations:**
The Arts Center on Brickyard Pond
Keene State College
Keene, NH

Janice Dolan   12

Peterborough, NH

Place of birth:
Peterborough, NH

Undergraduate:
University of New Hampshire,
Durham, NH

Graduate/continuing education:
Studio of Sidney F. Willis,
Bennington, NH

Art awards:
Catharine Lorillard Wolfe Award for
Painting, 1985
Fellowship, Virginia Center for
Creative Arts, 1986

Permanent collections:
Gurudev Siddha Peeth
Bombay, India

Major exhibitions:
Allied Artists
New York, NY

Catharine Lorillard Wolfe
New York, NY

Boston City Hall
Boston, MA

Gallery affiliation:
Portraits, Inc.
New York, NY

**Public/site-specific art work
locations:**
Health and Human Services Building
Concord, NH

Public Commission for World
Spiritual Leader
Chidvilasanda, India

John Terrence Downs   33

Rumney, NH

Place of birth:
Miami, FL
November 9, 1944

Undergraduate:
University of Miami, Miami, FL,
BA 1968

Graduate:
University of Miami, Miami, FL,
MA 1969
Florida State University, MFA 1971

Art awards:
The Currier Gallery of Art Award,
NHAA, 1981
Honorable Mention, Boston
Printmakers Association, 1985
Costello Memorial Award,
NHAA, 1984

Permanent collections:
Sceva Speare Hospital
Plymouth, NH

Academic Commons
Plymouth State College
Plymouth, NH

Arts Bank
State of New Hampshire

Major exhibitions:
One Man Show, 1984
Karl Drerup Gallery
Plymouth State College
Plymouth, NH

Portland Art Building, 1979
Portland, ME

Castleton State College, 1984
Castleton, VT

Gallery affiliation:
Horizons Art Gallery
Campton, NH

Current educational affiliation:
Plymouth State College
Associate of Art

**Public/site-specific art work
locations:**
NH Vocational-Technical College
Laconia, NH

Anne Dubois   10

Durham, NH

Place of birth:
Kansas City, MO
November 6, 1941

Undergraduate:
Grinnell College
Iowa State University
SUNY, Buffalo, NY, BA, cum laude

Graduate:
University of New Hampshire,
Durham, NH, MAT
Photography study with Dick
Merritt, UNH

Art awards:
First Prize, Jack Parfitt Memorial
Photography Exhibition, NH Art
Association, Manchester, NH, 1982
First Prize, Pro Portsmouth, 1984
Walt Kuhn Honorable Mention, 1981

Permanent collections:
Numerous private collections

Arts Bank
State of New Hampshire

Major exhibitions:
The Photographer, the Portrait &
the Environment, 1985
The Currier Gallery of Art
Manchester, NH

Theater by the Sea, 1984
Portsmouth, NH

League of NH Craftsmen Group
Show, 1984
Hanover, NH

Gallery affiliation:
Exeter Crafts Center
Exeter, NH

**Public/site-specific art work
locations:**
NH Vocational-Technical College
Stratham, NH

Irene E. DuPont 49

Manchester, NH

Place of birth:
Manchester, NH
November 11, 1938

Undergraduate:
Notre Dame College, Manchester,
NH, BA 1969

Art awards:
2nd Award, Jack Parfitt Memorial
Photography Exhibition, NH Art
Association, 1969

Permanent collections:
Pingree Art Museum
South Hamilton, MA

Corporate collections:
Nashua City Hall
Nashua, NH

Amoskeag Savings Bank
Manchester, NH

Memorial Hospital
Nashua, NH

Major exhibitions:
National Photo Show
West Virginia

National Juried Show
Ithaca, New York

NE Annual Juried Show
Millhouse-Bundy, Vermont

Gallery affiliations:
OUI Gallery
Boston, MA

Current educational affiliation:
Nashua Senior High School
Nashua, NH
Photography teacher

**Public/site-specific art work
locations:**
NH Council for the Humanities
Concord, NH

NH Vocational-Technical College
Stratham, NH

Catholic Medical Center
Manchester, NH

Jayne Dwyer 74

Portsmouth, NH

Place of birth:
Nashua, NH
August 1, 1928

Undergraduate:
Massachusetts College of Art,
Boston, MA, BS 1954

Graduate:
The Maryland Institute, College of
Art, Baltimore, MD, MFA 1970

Art awards:
NHAA, 1951, nine awards 1971-1979
National Award for Art At Your
Fingertips, Channel 11 TV Series,
1962-1963

Permanent collections:
Hundreds of works in private
collections

Arts Bank
State of New Hampshire

Major exhibitions:
One Woman Show, 1980
The Currier Gallery of Art
Manchester, NH

New England Drawing, 1979
DeCordova Museum
Lincoln, MA

American Drawings, 1979-1981
Smithsonian Traveling Exhibition

Current educational affiliation:
Ogunquit Art Association
Ogunquit, ME

Durham Art Association
Durham, NH

**Public/site-specific art work
locations:**
NH Vocational-Technical College
Laconia, NH

Katrena A. Earnest 25

La Palma, CA

Place of birth:
Atlanta, GA

Undergraduate:
Johnston College, University of
Redlands, CA, BA 1973

Graduate:
California State University, Long
Beach, CA, MFA Sculpture, 1981

Major exhibitions:
Interim, Chesterwood
Stockbridge, MA

New England Regional
University of Massachusetts
Amherst, MA

Current educational affiliation:
California State University Art
Department
Long Beach, CA
Lecturer

**Public/site-specific art work
locations:**
Health and Human Services Building
Concord, NH

Winslow Eaves 22

Potter Place, NH

Place of birth:
Detroit, MI
September 8, 1922

Undergraduate:
Cranbrook Art Academy, Bloomfield
Hills, MI, 1940-42
Studied with William Zorach, 1942-1943

Graduate:
The Beaux Arts, Paris, France

Art awards:
1st Sculpture Prize, NY International
Ceramics Exhibition, 1947
1st Sculpture Prize, NY Museum
Show, Rochester, NY, 1956, 1957
Commission for Robert Frost
Memorial Award Committee,
1979-1987

Permanent collections:
The Schenectady Museum
Schenectady, NY

Munson-Williams-Proctor Institute
Utica, NY

Syracuse University
Syracuse, NY

Corporate collections:
O K TOOL Company
Milford, NH

NH Savings Bank
Concord, NH

Major exhibitions:
U.S. Government European
Traveling Art Show

One Man Show
Fort Lauderdale Museum
Fort Lauderdale, FL

Gallery affiliation:
Kerygma Gallery
Allendale, NJ

**Public/site-specific art work
locations:**
NH State Library & Concord Hospital
Concord, NH

Plymouth State College
Plymouth, NH

Bill Finney 20

Hopkinton, NH

Place of birth:
Concord, NH
September 19, 1931

Education:
Self-taught

Art awards:
Kodak 1964-65 Worlds' Fair Colour
Award, 1965
The Currier Show Award, NHAA,
1968
1st Commercial Photographic Award,
Professional Photographers of New
England, 1967

Permanent collections:
The Currier Gallery of Art
Manchester, NH

Sandwich Historical Society
Sandwich, NH

Odiorne Park
State of New Hampshire
Rye, NH

Corporate collections:
First Capital Bank
Concord, NH

Major exhibitions:
The Currier Gallery of Art
Manchester, NH

Sandwich Historical Society
Sandwich, NH

Bermuda Art Association
Hamilton, Bermuda

**Public/site-specific art work
locations:**
Health and Human Services Building
Concord, NH

NH Vocational-Technical College
Manchester, NH

Norman Francoeur 21

Nashua, NH

Place of birth:
Nashua, NH
January 19, 1954

Undergraduate:
Franklin Institute of Photography,
Boston, MA, with Honors

Graduate/continuing education:
Building #18, Artist's complex,
Waltham, MA

Art awards:
Photographer of the Year, Creative
Division, NH Professional
Photographers Association, 1982
Best in Show, NH Professional
Photographers Association, 1981

Permanent collections:
Arts Bank
State of New Hampshire

Corporate collections:
Bay Banks
Middlesex Region, MA

Major exhibitions:
WET Gallery
Boston, MA

Gallery D.V.B
Boston, MA

WMAA Open Studios,
1986, 1987, 1988
Waltham, MA

Fall Exhibit, 1979, 1980, 1981
Nashua Artists Association
Nashua, NH

Fall Exhibit
American Stage Festival
Milford, NH

**Public/site-specific art work
locations:**
NH Vocational-Technical College
Stratham, NH

Light sculptures & designs for stage,
night clubs, films/videos

David Fullam 60

Newburyport, MA

Place of birth:
Princeton, NJ
July 27, 1945

Undergraduate:
Washington University School of
Fine Arts, St. Louis, MO, BFA 1969

Graduate:
Syracuse University School of Art,
Syracuse, NY, MFA 1972

Art awards:
Purchase Award, DeCordova
Museum, 1976
The Currier Gallery of Art Award,
NHAA 1985

Permanent collections:
DeCordova Museum
Lincoln, MA

Corporate collections:
Data Terminal Systems, Inc.
Acton, MA

First National Bank of Boston
Boston, MA

Northeast Electronics
Concord, NH

Major exhibitions:
New England Artists Under 36
DeCordova Museum
Lincoln, MA

New England Drawing and Traveling
Exhibit Competition
DeCordova Museum
Lincoln, MA

Gallery affiliation:
Clark Gallery
Lincoln, MA

Current educational affiliation:
Manchester Institute of Arts
& Sciences
Manchester, NH
Instructor in Painting

**Public/site-specific art work
locations:**
NH Vocational-Technical College
Manchester, NH

Dimitri Gerakaris 67

Canaan, NH

Place of birth:
Chicago, IL
December 25, 1947

Undergraduate:
Dartmouth College, Hanover, NH,
AB 1969

Art awards:
Golden Award, International
Institute of Iron Design, Aachen,
Germany, 1986
Alex W. Bezler Award, Artist-
Blacksmiths Association of North
America, 1987

Permanent collections:
Museum of Fine Arts
Boston, MA

British Artist-Blacksmiths
Association Collection
Coalbrookdale, England

National Ornamental Metalwork
Museum
Memphis, TN

Corporate collections:
W.C. Bradley Corporation
Columbus, GA

Opryland Hotel
Nashville, TN

Major exhibitions:
Smithsonian Institution
Washington, DC

International Exhibition of Wrought
Iron Sculptures
Lindau, Germany

Museum of Contemporary Crafts
New York, NY

Public/site-specific art work:
NH Vocational-Technical College
Manchester, NH

Boylston Place Gateway
Boston, MA

Rockefeller Center for the Social
Sciences
Hanover, NH

Eagle Square Gateway
Concord, NH

Dale M. Gottlieb 56

Bellingham, WA

Place of birth:
Brooklyn, NY
August 31, 1952

Undergraduate:
Art and Design College, Alfred
University, BFA 1975, Levins Award
in Painting

Major exhibitions:
Public School #122
New York, NY

Henry Street Settlement
New York, NY

Mink Brook Gallery
Lebanon, NH

**Public/site-specific art work
locations:**
Health and Human Services Building
Concord, NH

Kathy Hanson 50

Deerfield, NH

Place of birth:
Norwood, MA
May 4, 1944

Undergraduate:
University of Massachusetts,
Amherst, MA, BA 1966

Graduate:
Haystack Mt. School of Crafts,
Deer Isle, ME

Art awards:
Individual Artist Fellowship, NH
State Council on the Arts, 1983
Fellowship, Artists Foundation,
Boston, MA, 1986

Corporate collections:
Chubb LifeAmerica
Concord, NH

Home Bank
North Conway, NH

Major exhibitions:
Fairtree Gallery
New York, NY

Renwick Gallery
Smithsonian Institution
Washington, DC

Society of Arts and Crafts
Boston, MA

Gallery affiliation:
League of NH Craftsmen
Concord, NH

Current educational affiliation:
Artist-in-Residence Program
NH State Council on the Arts

**Public/site-specific art work
locations:**
NH State Prison
Concord, NH

Conley Harris 64

Boston, MA

Place of birth:
Clay Center, KS
July 7, 1943

Undergraduate:
University of Kansas, BFA 1965

Graduate:
University of Wisconsin, Madison,
WI, MFA 1965

Art awards:
Fellowship, Massachusetts Artists
Foundation, Boston, MA, 1986
Wurlitzer Foundation Residency,
Taos, NM, 1975

Permanent collections:
Museum of Fine Arts
Boston, MA

Fogg Art Museum
Cambridge, MA

Portland Museum of Art
Portland, ME

Corporate collections:
Fidelity Management and Research
Boston, MA

Metropolitan Life Insurance
New York, NY

Chubb LifeAmerica
Concord, NH

Major exhibitions:
Monique Knowlton Gallery
New York, NY

Singer Memorial Museum
Laren, Holland

Gallery affiliation:
Thomas Segal Gallery
Boston, MA

**Public/site-specific art work
locations:**
NH Vocational-Technical Colleges
Nashua & Stratham, NH

Health and Human Services Building
Concord, NH

Gannett Publishing Corporation
Washington, DC

Marie Harris 79

Barrington, NH

Place of birth:
New York, NY
November 7, 1943

Undergraduate:
Georgetown University School of
Foreign Service, 1961-1963
University of North Carolina,
1967-1968
Goddard College, Plainfield, VT,
BA 1971

Art awards:
Fellowship, National Endowment for
the Arts, 1976-1977
Individual Artist Fellowship, NH
State Council on the Arts, 1981
Golden Mike Award for "A Pride of
Writers," NH Association of
Broadcasters, 1981

Major exhibitions/publications:
Raw Honey, Alice James Books,
Cambridge, MA, 1975
Interstate, Slow Loris Press,
Pittsburgh, PA, 1980
*An Ear To The Ground: Toward A
Comprehensive U.S. Poetry Anthology*
(with Kathleen Aguero), University
of Georgia Press, Athens, GA, 1989

Current educational affiliation:
Artist-in-Residence Program
NH State Council on the Arts

**Public/site-specific art work
locations:**
Poem for Sunapee Mandala
Mount Sunapee State Park
NH Division of Parks & Recreation
Sunapee, NH

John W. Hatch 28

Durham, NH

Place of birth:
Saugus, MA
November 1, 1919

Undergraduate:
Massachusetts School of Art, 1941
Yale Fine Arts, BFA 1948

Graduate:
Yale University, MFA 1949

Art awards:
The Currier Gallery of Art Awards,
NHAA, 1949, 1956, 1958, 1961, 1976
1st Prize, Boston Watercolor Society,
1973, 1976

Permanent collections:
DeCordova Museum
Lincoln, MA

Addison Gallery of American Art
Andover, MA

Pennsylvania Academy of Fine Arts
Philadelphia, PA

Arts Bank
State of New Hampshire

Corporate collections:
Amoskeag National Bank & Trust
Company
Manchester, NH

Profile Savings Bank
Rochester, NH

Major exhibitions:
University of New Hampshire
Durham, NH

Addison Gallery
Andover, MA

Current educational affiliation:
University of New Hampshire
Professor, Emeritus

**Public/site-specific art work
locations:**
Supreme Court
Concord, NH

Health and Human Services Building
Concord, NH

Army Map Service Building
Washington, DC

Paul S. Howe 29

Sunapee, NH

Place of birth:
Raway, NJ
January 11, 1958

Education:
Self-taught

Art awards:
Honorable Mention, Photographer
Forum, 1980

Corporate collections:
GTE Sylvania
Massachusetts

Lake Sunapee Development
Corporation
New London, NH

Major exhibitions:
New London Hospital Day
New London, NH

Creative Arts Association of Andover
Andover, NH

Deming Gallery
New London, NH

**Public/site-specific art work
locations:**
NH Vocational-Technical College
Stratham, NH

Susan D. Howe 37

Manchester, NH

Place of birth:
New York, NY
December 6, 1945

Undergraduate:
Wheelock College, Boston, MA,
BS 1964

Graduate:
University of New Hampshire,
Durham, NH, Master in Ed. 1975
Manchester Institute of Arts &
Sciences, Manchester, NH Certificate
in Photography, 1986

Art awards:
NH Chapter American Institute of
Architects Photography Award,
NHAA, 1984, 1988
The Manchester Union Leader
Kodak Photography Award in
Color, 1986

Major exhibitions:
The League of NH Craftsmen
Annual Show, 1988
Durham, NH

"NH People at Work & Play"
Traveling Show, 1987-88
The Currier Gallery of Art
Manchester, NH

NHAA, 1987
Manchester, NH

**Public/site-specific art work
locations:**
NH Vocational-Technical College
Stratham, NH

Judith Inglese 65

Amherst, MA

Place of birth:
Takoma Park, MD
April 14, 1943

Undergraduate:
Sarah Lawrence College, Bronxville,
NY, BA 1965
Apprenticed with Clark Fitz-Gerald
and Paolo Soleri

Graduate:
Accademia di Belle Arti, Rome, Italy,
1963-1964
School of the Museum of Fine Arts,
Boston, MA 1968-1969

Art awards:
Craftsman's Award of Recognition,
Virginia American Institute of
Architects, 1983

Permanent collections:
National Zoological Park
Washington, DC

Maryland Municipal Swim Center
Rockville, MD

Numerous Public Schools
Maryland and New England

**Public/site-specific art work
locations:**
NH Vocational-Technical College
Nashua, NH

Lotte Jacobi 80
Concord, NH

Place of birth:
Thorn, West Prussia
August 17, 1896

Undergraduate:
Staatliche Höhere Fache-Schule:
für Phototechnik

Permanent collections:
Museum of Fine Arts
Boston, MA

Museum of Modern Art
New York, NY

Folkwang Museum
Essen, Germany

J. Paul Getty Museum
California

Arts Bank, illus. p. 80
State of New Hampshire

Numerous other collections in
Europe and America

Publications:
Lotte Jacobi, edited by Kelly Wise,
Addison House, Danbury, NH, 1978
*Lotte Jacobi, Russia 1932/33, Moskau,
Tadschikistan, Usbekistan*

Major exhibitions:
The Sense of Abstraction, 1960
Museum of Modern Art
New York, NY

Women of Photography,
An Historical Survey, 1975
San Francisco Museum of Art
San Francisco, CA

University of Chicago, 1965
Chicago, IL

Le Iven Salon National D'Art
Photographique, 1963
Blois, France

Current educational affiliation:
Honorary Degrees from the
University of New Hampshire,
Durham, NH, 1973 and New
England College, Henniker, NH, 1978

Peder Johnson 31
Nelson, NH

Place of birth:
Boston, MA
January 17, 1941

Undergraduate:
University of New Hampshire,
Durham, NH, BA 1963

Graduate:
University of Iowa, Iowa City, Iowa,
MA 1971

Permanent collections:
The Art Institute of Chicago
Chicago, IL

Arts Bank
State of New Hampshire

Corporate collections:
The MAC Group, Inc.
Cambridge, MA

Hotel Villa Parguera
Lajas, Puerto Rico

Major exhibitions:
Prince Street Gallery
New York, NY

XII Grand Prix International
d'Art Contemporaine
Monte Carlo, Monaco

Current educational affiliation:
Franklin Pierce College
Rindge, NH
Associate Professor

**Public/site-specific art work
locations:**
Health and Human Services Building
Concord, NH

William H. Johnson 32
Bristol, NH

Place of birth:
Lynn, MA
January 27, 1947

Undergraduate:
The Doscher Country School
of Photography, South Woodstock,
VT, 1974

Art awards:
Grand Prize, R&R Jewelry New
England Photo Contest, 1983
1st Prize, Arts Jubilee 14th Art
Show, 1986
Award of Merit, National
Cibachrome Photo Contest, 1980

Permanent collections:
Arts Bank
State of New Hampshire

Corporate collections:
Franklin Savings Bank
Bristol, NH

Major exhibitions:
The Craft of Photography
League of NH Craftsmen
Concord, NH

League of NH Craftsmen Annual
Exhibition
The Currier Gallery of Art
Manchester, NH

**Public/site-specific art work
locations:**
NH Vocational-Technical College
Stratham, NH

Kay Kandra 75
Nashua, NH

Place of birth:
Shamokin, PA
November 27, 1937

Undergraduate:
Philadelphia College of Art,
Philadelphia, PA, BFA w/honors,
1959

Graduate:
DeCordova Museum School,
1966-1970

Permanent collections:
Arts Bank
State of New Hampshire

US Department of Defense
Washington, DC

Corporate collections:
Chubb LifeAmerica
Concord, NH

Nashua Memorial Hospital
Nashua, NH

Major exhibitions:
NHAA
Manchester, NH

Arts Biennial
Manchester Institute of Arts and
Sciences
Manchester, NH

New England Watercolor Society
Boston, MA

Gallery affiliations:
McGowan Fine Art
Concord, NH

Priscilla Hartley
Kennebunkport, ME

**Public/site-specific art work
locations:**
NH Vocational-Technical College
Stratham, NH

Christopher Kressy   41
Plymouth, NH

Place of birth:
New York, NY
December 25, 1936

Undergraduate:
Rhode Island School of Design,
Providence, RI, BFA 1958

Graduate:
Yale University School of Art,
New Haven, CT, MFA 1964

Art awards:
Fulbright Exchange Grant,
1973-1974
Faculty Research Grant, University
of Massachusetts, 1966
First Prize, Painting—Pittsfield
Museum of Fine Arts, 1966

Permanent collections:
Addison Gallery of American Art
Andover, MA

University of Massachusetts
Amherst, MA

Franklin Pierce College
Concord, NH

Arts Bank
State of New Hampshire

Corporate collections:
Bain & Company
Boston, MA

Major exhibitions:
Triangle Show Soho
New York, NY

Althea Viafora Gallery
New York, NY

Alpha Gallery
Boston, MA

Current educational affiliation:
Plymouth State College
Plymouth, NH
Professor of Art

**Public/site-specific art work
locations:**
Health and Human Services Building
Concord, NH

Bob LaPree   62
Contoocook, NH

Place of birth:
Quantico, VA
December 16, 1947

Undergraduate:
New England College, Henniker,
NH, BA 1971

Art awards:
New Hampshire News Photographer
of Year, 1980

Permanent collections:
New England College Library
Henniker, NH

Corporate collections:
GTE Sylvania
Hillsboro, NH

Chubb LifeAmerica
Concord, NH

**Public/site-specific art work
locations:**
NH Vocational-Technical College
Stratham, NH

Steven Lee   51
Portsmouth, NH

Place of birth:
Jamestown, ND
April 3, 1952

Undergraduate:
University of North Dakota,
Grand Forks, ND, BA 1974

Graduate/continuing education:
Jagiellonski University, Krakow,
Poland, 1985

Major exhibitions:
Mural Works, 1985, 1986
The Button Factory
Portsmouth, NH

Five Portsmouth Artists
Portsmouth, NH

Gallery affiliation:
The Portsmouth Collection
Portsmouth, NH

**Public/site-specific art work
locations:**
New Hampshire State Prison
Concord, NH

New Hampshire Building/
NH Department of Agriculture
Eastern States Fairgrounds
West Springfield, MA

Christ the King Church
Ludlow, MA

Calvin J. Libby   69
Nashua, NH

Place of birth:
Barton, VT
June 22, 1931

Undergraduate:
New England School of Art, 1959

Art awards:
The Currier Prize, NHAA
Excellence in Abstract Painting,
Cape Cod Art Association
Sagendorph Award, Copley Society

Permanent collections:
Arts Bank
State of New Hampshire

Bristol Art Museum
Bristol, RI

Corporate collections:
Bank of New Hampshire
Nashua, NH

Amoskeag Bank
Manchester, NH

Shawmut Bank
Boston, MA

Major exhibitions:
DeCordova Museum
Lincoln, MA

Boston Fine Arts Festival
Boston, MA

St. Paul's School
Concord, NH

Gallery affiliation:
Kerygma Gallery
Ridgewood, NJ

Current educational affiliation:
Manchester Institute of Arts &
Sciences
Manchester, NH
Faculty, Graphic Design

**Public/site-specific art work
locations:**
NH State Prison
Concord, NH

Child & Family Services
Manchester, NH

NH Vocational-Technical College
Laconia, NH

Carol Travers Lummus 66

Barnstable, MA

Place of birth:
Hyannis, MA
November 2, 1937

Undergraduate:
Colby-Sawyer College, 1957
University of Geneva, Switzerland
Massachusetts College of Art,
Boston, MA

Art awards:
Colby-Sawyer College, 1957
Fitchburg Museum of Art, 1975
Rosmond DeKalb Award,
NHAA, 1975

Permanent collections:
University of Wisconsin
Madison, WI

American Red Cross
Boston, MA

Lund-Wassmer Museum
Salt Lake City, Utah

Major exhibitions:
National Association of
Women Artists
New York, NY

Saint-Gaudens National
Historic Site
Cornish, NH

National Cape Coral Annual
Cape Coral, FL

**Public/site-specific art work
locations:**
Health and Human Services Building
Concord, NH

Cabot Lyford 46

New Harbor, ME

Place of birth:
Sayre, PA
May 22, 1925

Undergraduate:
Cornell University, Ithaca, NY, BFA
Skowhegan School Sculpture Center,
Skowhegan, ME
Sculpture Center, New York, NY

Permanent collections:
Ogunquit Museum
Ogunquit, ME

Addison Gallery of Art
Andover, MA

Wichita Art Museum
Wichita, KS

Corporate collections:
Hitchiner Manufacturing
Milford, NH

Pneumo Corporation
Boston, MA

Ocean Spray Cranberries
Plymouth, MA

Major exhibitions:
The Addison Gallery of American Art
Andover, MA

The Lamont Gallery
Exeter, NH

Midtown Galleries
New York, NY

Gallery affiliation:
Midtown Galleries
New York, NY

**Public/site-specific art work
locations:**
NH Vocational-Technical College
Stratham, NH

Prescott and Albacore Parks
Portsmouth, NH

Regency Hotel
Portland, ME

Michael P. McConnell 59

Durham, NH

Place of birth:
Troy, Ohio
December 4, 1948

Undergraduate:
Ohio University, Athens, OH,
BFA 1970, summa cum laude

Graduate:
Ohio University, Athens, OH,
MFA 1974

Art awards:
Sculpture Award, Marietta College
International Competitive Exhibition,
Marietta, Ohio, 1976
Purchase Award, Award of Merit,
The Saenger National Jewelry and
Small Sculpture Exhibition, The
University of Southern Mississippi,
1978
Finalist, The International Sculpture
Competition, Johnson Atelier
Sculpture Institute, 1979

Permanent collections:
Butler Institute of American Art
Youngstown, OH

Laguna Gloria Art Museum
Austin, TX

The Currier Gallery of Art
Manchester, NH

Major exhibitions:
National Museum
Monaco

Superior Small Sculpture
San Diego, CA

On A Large Scale
The Currier Gallery of Art
Manchester, NH

Current educational affiliation:
University of New Hampshire
Durham, NH
Chair, Department of Art

**Public/site-specific art work
locations:**
Mercede City Center
Fort Lauderdale, FL

Health and Human Services Building
Concord, NH

Chase McNiss 23

Hudson, NH

Place of birth:
Lebanon, PA
April 6, 1951

Undergraduate:
New York Institute, Associate
Certificate of Photography, 1980

Graduate/continuing education:
Maine Photographic Workshops:
with Eliot Porter, 1983
Kodak Advanced Process
Management Program, Certificate
of Completion, 1982

Art awards:
2nd Place, Jack Parfitt Memorial
Photography Exhibition, NH Art
Association, 1987
NHAA 40th, 1986

Permanent collections:
Arts Bank
State of New Hampshire

Major exhibitions:
LaGrange National
LaGrange College
LaGrange, GA

Current occupation:
Commercial, Industrial and
Architectural Photographer
Nashua, NH

**Public/site-specific art work
locations:**
NH Vocational-Technical College
Stratham, NH

David Mendelsohn 13

Northwood, NH

Place of birth:
Anchorage, AK
February 3, 1951

Undergraduate:
Westchester College, AA 1975
Studied with Kipton Kummler,
Ernest Haas, and Jay Maisel

Art awards:
Communication Arts Art Annual,
1982, 1983, 1984
NH Chapter, American Institute of
Architects, NHAA, 1979

Permanent collections:
Clarence Kennedy Gallery
Boston, MA

Corporate collections:
Polaroid Corporation
Cambridge, MA

UNUM
Portland, ME

McKesson Corporation
San Francisco, CA

Major exhibitions:
Avenue Wagram Gallery
Paris, France

Pliubus Gallery
Tokyo, Japan

PPS Gallery
Hamburg, Germany

Gallery affiliation:
C.R. Fine Arts
Boston, MA

**Public/site-specific art work
locations:**
District of Columbia Community
Services
Washington, DC

Center for Humanistic Change
Washington, DC

Health and Human Services Building
Concord, NH

Thomas H. Meyers 71

Antrim, NH

Place of birth:
Poughkeepsie, NY
April 7, 1951

Undergraduate:
Rochester Institute of Technology,
New York, 1969-71
School of the Museum of Fine Arts,
Boston, MA, 1971-72
Architectural Glass Design Seminars
w/ Ludwig Schaffrath

Art awards:
Individual Artist Fellowship, NH
State Council on the Arts, 1986
Best of Show, Annual Juried Exhibit,
Sharon Arts Center, 1985

Permanent collections:
Arts Bank
State of New Hampshire

Corporate collections:
Saint Joseph Hospital Chapel
Nashua, NH

Saint Theresa Parish
Rye, NH

Major exhibitions:
Collage & Masks
Sharon Arts Center
Sharon, NH

Fifty States Exhibition
Traverse City, MI

Artist and the Object
The Chapel Arts Center
Saint Anselm College
Manchester, NH

Gallery affiliation:
Fine Art Resources, Inc.
New York, NY

**Public/site-specific art work
locations:**
NH Vocational-Technical College
Stratham, NH

Peter W. Milton 73

Francestown, NH

Place of birth:
Lower Merion, PA
April 2, 1930

Undergraduate:
Yale University, New Haven, CT,
BFA 1954, Yale Traveling Fellowship

Graduate:
Yale University, New Haven, CT,
MFA 1961

Permanent collections:
Metropolitan Museum of Art
New York, NY

Museum of Modern Art
New York, NY

Tate Gallery of Art
London, England

Gallery affiliation:
Franz Bader Gallery
Washington, DC

**Public/site-specific art work
locations:**
NH Vocational-Technical College
Laconia, NH

Patti Mitchem 70

South Berwick, ME

Place of birth:
Rangely, CO
June 1, 1952

Undergraduate:
University of Colorado, Boulder, CO
Workshop with Jack Lenor Larson
and Randall Darwall, 1984

Art awards:
Best in Show, 3rd New Hampshire
Crafts Biennial, Manchester Institute
of Arts and Sciences, Manchester, NH
Best in Wallhangings and Popular
Choice, New England Weaver's
Seminar Exhibition
Governor's Purchase Award, Illinois
State Fair Professional Art Show

Permanent collections:
Illinois State Museum
Springfield, IL

Corporate collections:
Harris Graphics
Dover, NH

Chubb LifeAmerica
Concord, NH

IBM
Bedford, NH; Burlington, VT;
Boca Raton, FL

Major exhibitions:
New England Fiber Arts
Newport Art Museum
Newport, RI

Makers '86
Maine Crafts Association Annual
Juried Exhibition
Brunswick, ME

Gallery affiliation:
McGowan Fine Art
Concord, NH

**Public/site-specific art work
locations:**
NH Vocational-Technical College
Nashua, NH

NYNEX Information Services
Lynn, MA

Bank of New Hampshire
Concord, NH

| **Frank Moulton** 40 | **Judith Wilbour Nelson** 61 | **Sylvia Nicolas O'Neill** 35 | **Sherry Palmer** 36 |

Frank Moulton — 40
Portsmouth, NH

Place of birth:
Boston, MA
March 5, 1927

Undergraduate:
Dartmouth College, Hanover, NH,
BA 1950, Magna Cum Laude,
Phi Beta Kappa

Art awards:
First Prize, Hopkins Center Exhibit,
Dartmouth, NH, 1973
First Prize: Friends of Acapulco
International, Mexico, 1974
The Currier Gallery Award of Art,
NHAA, 1988

Permanent collections:
Ogunquit Art Museum
Ogunquit, ME

Palace of Fine Arts
Fortakza, Ceana, Brazil

Supreme Court
Concord, NH

Arts Bank
State of New Hampshire

Corporate collections:
John Deere International
Moline, IL

**Public/site-specific art work
locations:**
NH Vocational-Technical College
Stratham, NH

Judith Wilbour Nelson — 61
Little Compton, RI

Place of birth:
Manchester, NH
April 1, 1951

Undergraduate:
Rhode Island School of Design,
Providence, RI, BFA 1976, Honors
3-D design

Graduate:
Cranbrook Academy of Art,
Bloomfield Hills, MI, MFA 1978,
Merit Scholarship

Art awards:
Best of Show, League of NH
Craftsmen Exhibition, 1977

Corporate collections:
IBM Headquarters
Armonk, NY

Sheraton Corporation
Los Angeles, CA

National Fire Protection Agency
Quincy, MA

Major exhibitions:
Young Americans
Museum of Contemporary Crafts
New York, NY

Fiber National
Downey Museum
Downey, CA

New England Fiber Show
Boston City Hall
Boston, MA

**Public/site-specific art work
locations:**
NH Technical Institute
Concord, NH

Sylvia Nicolas O'Neill — 35
Mont Vernon, NH

Place of birth:
Schoorl, Netherlands
May 24, 1928

Undergraduate:
Academie de la Grand Chamiere,
Paris, France, 1951
Academie Julien, Paris, France,
1949-1951
Studied with Rufino Tamayo, 1945

Graduate:
Institut Des Hautes Etudes
Cinematographique, Paris, France

Permanent collections:
Netherlands Government
Netherlands

Church of Annunciation
Washington, DC

Marienspital
Dusseldorf, Germany

Saint Anselm Abbey
Manchester, NH

Major exhibitions:
Museum Albert Kuyder
Roermond, Netherlands

Chapel Art Center
Saint Anselm College
Manchester, NH

Nashua Arts and Science Center
Nashua, NH

**Public/site-specific art work
locations:**
Health and Human Services Building
Concord, NH

Saint Pancratius
Tubbergen, Netherlands
Four Generations Foundation thus
completing a church which already
possessed windows by great-
grandfather, grandfather, and father.

Stained glass in schools, hospitals,
retirement homes, churches,
monasteries, offices in the Netherlands

Bronze sculptures and mosaics at
Saint Anselm College, Manchester, NH

Sherry Palmer — 36
Dover, NH

Place of birth:
Gardner, ME
January 2, 1947

Undergraduate:
University of New Hampshire,
Durham, NH, BA 1969

Graduate:
University of New Hampshire,
Durham, NH, MAT 1974

Permanent collections:
Union Mutual
Portland, ME

Major exhibitions:
Alumni Revisited
University of New Hampshire
Durham, NH

4-Women Show
The Gallery
Portsmouth, NH

2-Person Show, 1986
PS Gallery
Ogunquit, ME

5 Artists
Walt Kuhn Gallery
Cape Neddick, ME

Gallery affiliation:
PS Gallery
Ogunquit, ME

The Cape Neddick Inn and Gallery
Cape Neddick, ME

**Public/site-specific art work
locations:**
NH Vocational-Technical College
Stratham, NH

<table>
<tr><td>

Loran D. Percy   68
Lakeport, NH

Place of birth:
Laconia, NH
June 10, 1931

Art awards:
Best of Show, Laconia Art
Association, 1988

Permanent collections:
Over 2000 works in private and
public collections

Corporate collections:
Village Bank
Gilford, NH

Irwin Motors
Laconia, NH

Franklin Savings Bank
Franklin, NH

Gallery affiliation:
Ashbrook Gallery
Wolfeboro and Meredith, NH

**Public/site-specific art work
locations:**
Post Office Lobby
Laconia, NH

Gunstock Ski Area
Gilford, NH

NH State Prison
Concord, NH

</td><td>

Paul Pollaro   44
Hancock, NH

Place of birth:
New York, NY
August 2, 1921

Undergraduate:
Art Students League, New York, NY

Graduate:
Pratt Graphic Center

Art awards:
2nd Prize, Jersey City Museum, 1966
MacDowell Colony Fellowship,
1965, 67, 68, 69
Individual Artist Fellowship, NH
State Council on the Arts, 1985

Permanent collections:
Museum of New Mexico
Santa Fe, NM

Staten Island Museum
New York, NY

The Currier Gallery of Art
Manchester, NH

Corporate collections:
IBM
Bedford, NH

Bank of New Hampshire
Manchester, NH

Continental Can Company
New York, NY

Major exhibitions:
Phillips Exeter Academy
Exeter, NH

Manchester Institute of Arts
and Sciences
Manchester, NH

Staten Island Museum
New York, NY

Gallery affiliations:
Michael Dunev Gallery
San Francisco, CA

Franz Bader Gallery
Washington, DC

**Public/site-specific art work
locations:**
NH Vocational-Technical College
Stratham, NH

</td><td>

Peter E. Randall   9
Hampton, NH

Place of birth:
Newburyport, MA
November 12, 1940

Undergraduate:
University of New Hampshire,
Durham, NH

Permanent collections:
Arts Bank
State of New Hampshire

Audubon Society of New Hampshire
Concord, NH

Major exhibitions/publications:
A Stern and Lovely Scene, 1978
University Art Galleries
University of New Hampshire
Durham, NH

The Currier Gallery of Art
Manchester, NH

*New Hampshire Four Seasons
All Creation and the Isles of Shoals
Portsmouth and the Piscataqua*

Educational affiliation:
Winnacunnet High School
Hampton, NH
Adult Education Program

Shoals Marine Laboratory
Appledore Island, ME
Instructor, Nature Photography

**Public/site-specific art work
locations:**
NH Vocational-Technical College
Stratham, NH

</td><td>

Gary Samson   11
Concord, NH

Place of birth:
Manchester, NH
June 30, 1951

Undergraduate:
Franklin Institute, Boston, MA,
Photography Degree, 1971

Art awards:
Boston Film and Video Foundation,
1983
Award for Photography, New
Hampshire Arts Biennial, 1985
First Place Award, The Connecticut
Film Festival, *Lotte Jacobi: A Film
Portrait, 1980*

Permanent collections:
Arts Bank
State of New Hampshire

The Currier Gallery of Art
Manchester, NH

University of NH Art Galleries
Durham, NH

Major exhibitions:
The Lithuanians of Nashua, NH
The Currier Gallery of Art
Manchester, NH

Manchester Historic Association
Manchester, NH

AVA Gallery
Hanover, NH

Gallery affiliation:
New Hampshire Art Association
Manchester, NH

Current educational affiliation:
Manchester Institute of Arts
and Sciences
Manchester, NH
Chairman and Instructor,
Photography Department

**Public/site-specific art work
locations:**
Health and Human Services Building
Concord, NH

NH Vocational-Technical College
Manchester, NH

</td></tr>
</table>

Lee A. Schuette   58
Portsmouth, NH

Place of birth:
Berlin, NH
August 2, 1951

Undergraduate:
University of New Hampshire,
Durham, NH, BFA 1973

Graduate:
Rhode Island School of Design,
Providence, RI, MFA 1981

Art awards:
Graduate Fellowship, Rhode Island
School of Design, 1980-81
Judges Award, Young Americans,
American Crafts Council, 1977
Fellowship, National Endowment for
the Arts, 1976

Corporate collections:
Hechinger Corporation
Richmond, VA

Mittleman Design
New York, NY

Steinway Piano
Long Island, NY

Major exhibitions:
One Man Show, 1988
Milliken Gallery
New York, NY

American Furniture Past and Present
Society of Arts and Crafts and
Boston Museum of Fine Arts
Boston, MA

The School of Wendell Castle
Snyderman Gallery
Philadelphia, PA

Gallery affiliation:
Milliken Gallery
New York, NY

**Public/site-specific art work
locations:**
New Hampshire Hospital
Concord, NH

League of NH Craftsmen Store
and Educational Center
North Conway, NH

Julie S. Serrano   18
Alton, NH

Place of birth:
Rochester, NY
January 13, 1940

Undergraduate:
University of New Hampshire,
Durham, NH, 1973-1981

Graduate:
Lesley College Graduate School,
Cambridge, MA, MA 1984

Art awards:
Individual Artist Fellowship, New
Hampshire State Council on the
Arts, 1981

Permanent collections:
Arts Bank
State of New Hampshire

Major exhibitions:
The Nursing Home Suite, 1982
John F. Kennedy Building
Boston, MA

Social Concerns of the '80's, 1984
Boston University
Boston, MA

The Indignant Artist
Plymouth State College
Plymouth, NH

**Public/site-specific art work
locations:**
Health and Human Services Building
Concord, NH

Eric F. Sinclair   14
Dover, NH

Place of birth:
Exeter, NH
August 8, 1953

Undergraduate:
University of New Hampshire,
Durham, NH, BS 1975

Permanent collections:
Arts Bank
State of New Hampshire

Major exhibitions:
The Inn Street Gallery
Newburyport, MA

The Water Street Gallery
Exeter, NH

Current educational affiliation:
Phillips Exeter Academy
Exeter, NH
Instructor of Music, Guitar

**Public/site-specific art work
locations:**
NH Vocational-Technical College
Stratham, NH

Richard T. Slater   39
Contoocook, NH

Place of birth:
Poughkeepsie, NY
October 6, 1948

Art awards:
Black & White Portrait, NH
Professional Photographers
Association, 1986

Permanent collections:
Arts Bank
State of New Hampshire

Sprague Energy
Portsmouth, NH

**Public/site-specific art work
locations:**
NH Vocational-Technical College
Stratham, NH

| **Gary Haven Smith** 34 | **Todd Smith** 19 | **M. Patricia Splaine** 51 | **Jo Ann Stover** 42 |

Gary Haven Smith   34
Barnstead, NH

Place of birth:
Boston, MA
December 7, 1948

Undergraduate:
University of New Hampshire,
Durham, NH, BFA 1973, David
Campbell Prize

Art awards:
Individual Artist Fellowship, NH
State Council on the Arts, 1985
Paul Costello Award, NHAA, 1986
The Hitchiner Award, NHAA, 1985

Corporate collections:
CIGNA Corporation
Wilmington, DE

NYNEX
Washington, DC

General Electric Company
Fairfield, CT

Major exhibitions:
Blackthorn Gallery
Portsmouth, NH

Process
The Chapel Arts Center
Saint Anselm College
Manchester, NH

Seasons Gallery
The Hague, Netherlands

**Public/site-specific art work
locations:**
Walt Kuhn Park
Cape Neddick, ME

NH Technical Institute
Concord, NH

Todd Smith   19
Concord, NH

Place of birth:
Detroit, MI
January 27, 1947

Undergraduate:
Pratt Institute, New York, NY,
BA 1968, Cum Laude

Graduate:
Pratt Institute, New York, NY,
MFA 1972

Art awards:
Print Magazine National Design
Annual Award, 1986
New England Museum Association
Award, Poster Design, 1986
American Association of Museums,
1st Prize for Publications, 1986

Permanent collections:
Brooklyn Museum
New York, NY

The Agnelli Collection
Milan, Italy

The Klein Collection
New York, NY

Major exhibitions:
Focus Gallery
Detroit, MI

10 Downtown
New York, NY

League of NH Craftsmen
Concord, NH

**Public/site-specific art work
locations:**
Health and Human Services Building
Concord, NH

M. Patricia Splaine   51
Portsmouth, NH

Place of birth:
Peabody, MA
December 21, 1946

Undergraduate:
University of New Hampshire,
Durham, NH

Art awards:
Organization of the Year Award, Pro
Portsmouth, Portsmouth, NH, 1983

Permanent collections:
Christ the King Church
Ludlow, MA

Corporate collections:
Ken McVicur
Venture Capital
Mansfield, MA

**Public/site-specific art work
locations:**
The Children's Museum of
Portsmouth
Portsmouth, NH

Gilly's Diner
Portsmouth, NH

NH State Prison
Concord, NH

Jo Ann Stover   42
Keene, NH

Place of birth:
Peterborough, NH

Undergraduate:
New England College of Art,
Boston, MA, 1949-53
Massachusetts School of Art,
Boston, MA, 1954
Art Students League, New York,
NY 1954-55

Art awards:
First Prize, City Center Gallery,
New York, NY, 1955
Honorable Mention, National
Academy of Arts & Design,
New York, NY, 1956
Junior Literary Guild Award for
3 Children's Books, Writing and
Illustration, 1961-62

Permanent collections:
Kerlan Collection
University of Minnesota

New England Telephone Company
Manchester, NH

Major exhibitions:
Blackthorn Gallery
Portsmouth, NH

Gallery affiliations:
Patrone
Cape Porpoise, ME

The Greenhut
Portland, ME

Gallery on the Green
Lexington, MA

**Public/site-specific art work
locations:**
Health and Human Services
Building
Concord, NH

Chuck Theodore 38

Franconia, NH

Place of birth:
Manchester, NH
March 6, 1949

Undergraduate:
University of New Hampshire,
Durham, NH, 1972 Philosophy

Permanent collections:
Arts Bank
State of New Hampshire

130 Libraries throughout
New England

Corporate collections:
The Savers Bank
Plymouth & Lincoln, NH

Sheraton Inn
South Portland, ME

Bigelow & Company
Manchester, NH

Gallery affiliation:
Rivendell Gallery of Fine
Art Photography
Franconia, NH

**Public/site-specific art work
locations:**
NH Youth Development Center
Manchester, NH

Laconia State School
Laconia, NH

Glencliff Home for the Elderly
Glencliff, NH

NH Vocational-Technical College
Stratham, NH

Janis E. Theodore 52

Boston, MA

Place of birth:
Manchester, MA
April 22, 1947

Undergraduate:
University of New Hampshire,
Durham, NH, BFA 1974, Campbell
Scholarship

Graduate:
Indiana University, Bloomington,
IN, MFA 1976, Graduate Fellowship

Art awards:
Best of Show, Fine Arts Center,
Taos, NM, 1985
First Prize, Galex 18, International
Exhibition, Galesburg, IL, 1984
Eberhard Faber, Inc. Award, The
Pastel Society of America, NY, NY

Permanent collections:
Arts Bank
State of New Hampshire

Washington & Jefferson College
Washington, PA

Corporate collections:
Hale & Dorr
Boston, MA

Major exhibitions:
Manchester Institute of Arts
& Sciences
Manchester, NH

Jersey City State College
Jersey City, NJ

Salem State College
Salem, MA

Gallery affiliation:
Uptown Gallery
New York, NY

Current educational affiliation:
Smith College
Northampton, MA
Asst. Prof., Drawing/Design

**Public/site-specific art work
locations:**
Health and Human Services Building
Concord, NH

Esther Amelia Titcomb 63

Deering, NH

Place of birth:
Boston, MA
June 15, 1918

Undergraduate:
Self-taught and New England College
Harvard University, and studied
with Lotte Jacobi

Art awards:
Best of Show, Manchester Institute
of Arts & Sciences, Manchester,
NH 1975
First Prizes, NHAA, 1970's

Permanent collections:
Arts Bank
State of New Hampshire

Corporate collections:
Granite Hill Industries
Hooksett, NH

Bank of New Hampshire
Manchester, NH

Windsor Nurseries
Windham, NH

Major exhibitions/publications:
Women In History
New Hampshire State House
Concord, NH

One Woman Show
New England College
Henniker, NH

Two Woman Show, 1975
NH Commission on the Arts
Concord, NH

Published in *Helicon NINE*,
Summer, 1986

**Public/site-specific art work
locations:**
NH Vocational-Technical College
Stratham, NH

S.C. Valastro 48

Indian Lake, NY

Place of birth:
New York, NY
April 24, 1922

Undergraduate:
Pratt Institute, New York, NY,
Bachelor in Architecture, 1950

Graduate:
Ecole Beaux Arts, Fontainebleau,
France, Prix Remondet, Design, 1950

Art awards:
First Prize, Architectural Photography,
American Institute of Architects,
Washington, DC, 1957
Third Prize, Color, Photography
International Exhibition (over
73,000 entries) 1952
Purchase Award, 1st Annual
Photographic Competition, Walt
Kuhn Gallery, Cape Neddick,
ME, 1981

Permanent collections:
Photography and Library Department
Museum of Modern Art
New York, NY

George Eastman House
Rochester, NY

DeCordova Museum
Lincoln, MA

Corporate collections:
Memorial Bridge Commission
Portsmouth, NH

Chubb Group, Inc.
Pittsburgh, PA

National Life Insurance Co.
Lincoln, MA

Current educational affiliation:
Indian Lake Central School
Indian Lake, NY
Volunteer, Mentor Program,
Architecture & Photography

**Public/site-specific art work
locations:**
NH Vocational-Technical College
Stratham, NH

Herbert O. Waters   30
Campton, NH

Place of birth:
Shantou, China
November 15, 1903

Undergraduate:
Denison University, Granville, OH,
Ph.B. 1926 Phi Beta Kappa

Graduate:
Harvard University, Cambridge, MA
1932-33
Art Institute of Chicago, 1928-31

Art awards:
Society of American Graphic
Artists, New York, NY, 1955
Appalachian Corridors II Exhibit,
Charleston, WV, 1970

Permanent collections:
Metropolitan Museum of Art
New York, NY

Boston Public Library
Boston, MA

Library of Congress
Washington, DC

Major exhibitions:
Metropolitan Museum of Art
New York, NY

New York World's Fair, 1939

Society of Wood Engravers, 1988
London, England

Gallery affiliation:
Mary Ryan Gallery
New York, NY

Old Print Barn
Meredith, NH

Current educational affiliation:
Honorary Doctor of Fine Arts, 1985
Alderson-Broaddus College
Philippi, WV

Honorary Doctor of Fine Arts, 1984
Plymouth State College
Plymouth, NH

**Public/site-specific art work
locations:**
NH Vocational-Technical College
Laconia, NH

Anne C. Weber   53
Durham, NH

Place of birth:
Berwyn, IL
January 30, 1937

Undergraduate:
University of New Hampshire,
Durham, NH, BFA 1982

Permanent collections:
Arts Bank
State of New Hampshire

Corporate collections:
Congoleum Corporation
Portsmouth, NH

Major exhibitions:
Academic Artist Association
National Juried Exhibition
Springfield, MA

Gallery affiliation:
Vaughn Gallery
Portsmouth, NH

**Public/site-specific art work
locations:**
Health and Human Services Building
Concord, NH

D. Cary Wendell   51
Portsmouth, NH

Place of birth:
Bryn Mawr, PA
June 19, 1950

Undergraduate:
Haverford College, Haverford, PA,
BA 1972

Graduate:
School of the Museum of Fine Arts,
Boston, MA

Permanent collection:
Haverford College
Haverford, PA

Banff Center School of Fine Art
Banff, Alberta, Canada

**Public/site-specific art work
locations:**
The Manchester Mural
Manchester, NH

NH Savings Bank
Concord, NH

Market Square Mural
Portsmouth, NH

NH State Prison
Concord, NH

New Hampshire Building/NH
Department of Agriculture
Eastern States Fairgrounds
West Springfield, MA

Fleur Weymouth   47
Jaffrey, NH

Undergraduate:
Vassar College, BA in Philosophy,
1957

Permanent collections:
Arts Bank
State of New Hampshire

Major exhibitions:
One Woman Show
Morris Gallery
New York, NY

Berkshire Museum
Pittsfield, MA

Photographers' Gallery
Sanibel Island, FL

Current occupation:
Photography Editor
Helicon NINE:
The Journal of Women's Arts Letters

**Public/site-specific art work
locations:**
NH Vocational-Technical College
Stratham, NH

Center Harbor, ME

Place of birth:
New Castle, IN
December 1, 1932

Undergraduate:
Purdue University, BA 1955

Graduate:
Columbia University, MA 1959

Permanent collections:
Library of Congress
Washington, DC

Museum of Fine Arts
Boston, MA

Museum of Fine Arts
Houston, TX

Corporate collections:
Bank of Boston
Boston, MA

Polaroid Corporation
Cambridge, MA

Educational affiliation:
Phillips Andover Academy
Andover, MA

**Public/site-specific art work
locations:**
Health and Human Services Building
Concord, NH

ACKNOWLEDGMENTS

During the tenth year of the Percent for Art Program, the
New Hampshire State Council on the Arts wishes to publicly
acknowledge and thank the many volunteers who have
contributed their time, knowledge, and perspectives on
behalf of the arts in New Hampshire. The Council also
wishes to praise the thoughtfulness of those who created
and supported the initiating legislation and shaped the
guidelines which charted the course of the first 10 years.
The program has grown and found definition thanks to the
spirit of cooperation shared by all of the many people who
gave of themselves to make the individual projects happen.

Tenth Anniversary Steering Committee
Helen P. Closson, Chair; Shirley Gray Adamovich; Susan Bonaiuto; Edith Grodin; Rebecca L. Lawrence; James Locke; Gary Samson; Gary Haven Smith; Audrey V. Sylvester; Mary C. Taylor. Special thanks to Helen Closson for raising private donations for the publication.

Sponsors of Percent for Art Legislation
Elaine Krasker, Prime Sponsor; James V. Bibbo, Jr.; Mary P. Chambers; Marshall French; Ruth Griffin; Mary Louise Hancock; Peter C. Hildreth; Paul I. LaMott; Vesta M. Roy.

Percent for Art Task Force
David Batchelder, Mel Bolden, Grace Casey, Sara Germain, Delnoce Goubert, Calvin J. Libby, Nancy Lyon, Walter Mead, Mary Lyn Ray, Susan Taylor.

New Hampshire Governors
(During the Ten-year Period, 1979-1989)
Hugh J. Gallen, John H. Sununu, Judd Gregg

Commissioner, Department of Libraries, Arts and Historial Resources
Shirley Gray Adamovich

New Hampshire State Arts Agency Directors
(During the Ten-year Period, 1979-1989)
John G. Coe, Ann Backus (Acting Director), Robb Hankins, Susan Bonaiuto.

Percent for Art Program Coordinators
Susan Taylor, 1979-1981; Audrey V. Sylvester, 1981-present.

Commissioners/Council Members who served on Art Selection Committees
Patricia Bass, Cynthia Beebe, Helen P. Closson, Barbara B. Dunfey, Edith Grodin, James Locke, Dorothy Pearlstein, Kenneth Spritz, James W. Tebbetts, Helen Winebaum.

Art Selection Committee Members
Maureen Ahern, Sharon Amberger, David Batchelder, Doris Birmingham, Ralph Brickett, Roger Dignard, Robert M. Doty, Robert Dowst, Katrena A. Earnest, Alan L. Erdossy, Joan Esch, Elizabeth Gurrier, Sarah Haskell, Louise Kalin, Elaine Krasker, Elizabeth Rowland Mayor, Allan P. McCulloch, Mary Strayer McGowan, Walter Mead, Richard Monahon, Charles Oliver, Paul Pollaro, Angelo Randazzo, Mary Lyn Ray, Helen K. Reid, Peter Sabin, Gary Samson, Philip Tambling, Mary C. Taylor, Annette Tischler, Harry Umen, Leslie Voiers, Newt Washburn, Christopher P. Williams, Bliss Woodruff.

Mount Sunapee State Park, Sunapee; New Hampshire Division of Parks and Recreation: Richard Antonia, Ruth Burt, Judy Cummings, Wilbur LaPage, Judy Northup-Bennett, Debbie Sias, Kathleen Soldati, Malcolm Thomas, Bill Ulinski.

Site Advisory Committees The Arts Center on Brickyard Pond, Keene State College, Keene:
Maureen Ahern, Samuel Azzaro, David Clark, Richard Cunningham, Tom Iovanne, "Babs" Putnam, Erika Radich, Judith A. Sturnick, Paul Vincent, Susan Wirth. And special thanks to George Kovacs; Robert L. Mallet, Jr.; Leandre Poisson; and Tony Tremblay.

Health and Human Services Building (formerly Health and Welfare, Concord): Laurie Cullerot, Robert Deitchi-Cooper, Sylvio Dupuis, Ned Helms, Tom Korst, Ted Lewis, April Munson, Susie Reid.

New Hampshire Fish and Game Department, Concord: John S. Bowyer, Jr.; Allen F. Crabtree, III; Patricia R. Fleurie; John W. Merkle; Donald A. Normandeau; James Paine; Ellen Rice; Ron Ruffle; Judy Silverberg; Joseph J. Walsh.

New Hampshire Hospital, Concord: Ann Anderson, Chester Batchelder, Jaye Cate, Michael Lassel, Richard C. Lippincott, Barbara Maloney, Jack E. Melton, Phyllis Stibler.

New Hampshire State Library, Concord: Shirley Gray Adamovich, Jean Johnson, Judy Kimball, Clare Ryan, Stella Scheckter, William Winston Smith.

New Hampshire State Prison, Concord: Mike Angelli, Dick Ashley, Michael Cunningham, Lt. Louis Dall, Richard Dudley, Peter McDonald, David Page, Everett Perrin, Nicholas Pishon, Bob Scarborough.

New Hampshire Technical Institute, Concord: Margaret Alix; Barry Brensigner; Lisa DeStefano; William John Hare; Paul Hemmerich; David E. Larrabee, Sr.; Everett Munson; Jim Sindelar; Elaine Scovill; Janet Talbot; John Tunney.

New Hampshire Vocational-Technical College, Laconia; Ray LaPointe, Robert Turner.

New Hampshire Vocational-Technical College, Manchester: Richard E. Mandeville, Mark Normand, Thomas A. Wallace.

New Hampshire Vocational-Technical College, Nashua: Robert Bloomfield, William McIntyre, David Page, Warren Quaine, Marie Sias.

New Hampshire Vocational-Technical College, Stratham: Kenneth Coombs, Dale Dollar, Nan Fahey, Charles Green, Sue Malcolm, Barney Stone, David Veno.

Upham-Walker House, Concord, Office Space Study Committee on Capital Planning: James V. Bibbo, Jr.; George Freese; Paul LaMott; Lee Marden; Susan McLane; Walter Mead; Elizabeth Murphy; Bruce Rounds; John Stabile; Robert Steven; John B. Tucker; and Sy Vershon.

The New Hampshire State Council on the Arts wishes to acknowledge the donors who made generous contributions to the following Percent for Art projects.

Project: "Sunapee Mandala," Emile Birch, Mount Sunapee State Park.
Donors: John Swenson Granite Company, Inc.; Lake Sunapee Business Association; League of New Hampshire Craftsmen Foundation, Inc.; New Hampshire Division of Parks and Recreation.

Project: "Athanor," Jean-Denis Cruchet, The Arts Center on Brickyard Pond.
Donor: "Investments in Quality—The Campaign for Keene State College."

Project: "Teahouse Pavillion," Lee A. Schuette and associate, Rick McAulay, New Hampshire Hospital.
Donors: Peter Bosiak; Corriveau-Routhier, Inc.; Fletcher Granite Company, Inc.; John Swenson Granite Company, Inc.; Darald R. and Juliet Libby.

To all who testified on behalf of the legislation; to all the maintenance crews who have protected and monitored the artwork; and last, but not least, to all the artists whose talents, imagination, and hard work have made Percent for Art possible, the Council extends its thanks.

**The Arts Center on
Brickyard Pond**
Keene State College
Keene, NH

**Health and Human Services
Building**
(formerly Health and Welfare
Building)
6 Hazen Drive
Concord, NH

Mount Sunapee State Park
New Hampshire Division of Parks
and Recreation
Sunapee, NH

**New Hampshire Fish and
Game Department**
2 Hazen Drive
Concord, NH

New Hampshire Hospital
105 Pleasant Street
Concord, NH

New Hampshire State Library
20 Park Street
Concord, NH

New Hampshire State Prison
281 North State Street
Concord, NH

**New Hampshire Technical
Institute**
The Tech Center
Institute Drive
Concord, NH

**New Hampshire Vocational-
Technical College**
Prescott Hill
Laconia, NH

**New Hampshire Vocational-
Technical College**
1066 Front Street
Manchester, NH

**New Hampshire Vocational-
Technical College**
505 Amherst Street
Nashua, NH

**New Hampshire Vocational-
Technical College**
277 R. Portsmouth Avenue
Stratham, NH

Upham-Walker House
18 Park Street
Concord, NH